Bible

Books by Ivor Powell

Bible Cameos
Bible Gems
Bible Highways
Bible Names of Christ
Bible Nuggets
Bible Pinnacles
Bible Treasures
Bible Windows
Matthew's Majestic Gospel
Mark's Superb Gospel
Luke's Thrilling Gospel
John's Wonderful Gospel
The Amazing Acts
The Exciting Epistle to the Ephesians
What in the World Will Happen Next?
David: His Life and Times

Bible Nuggets

Treasures of Truth from the World's Richest Storehouse

Ivor Powell

KREGEL PUBLICATIONS
Grand Rapids, Michigan 49501

Bible Nuggets, by Ivor Powell. © 1991 by Kregel Publications, a division of Kregel, Inc., P. O. Box 2607, Grand Rapids, Michigan 49501. All rights reserved.

Cover Design: Don Ellens
Cover Photo: Art Jacobs

Library of Congress Cataloging-in-Publication Data

Powell, Ivor, 1910-
  Bible Nuggets.
    p.   cm.
  Includes index.
  1. Sermons—Outlines, syllabi, etc. I. Title.
BS4223.P685   1991   251'.02—dc20   91-24340
                                                    CIP

ISBN   0-8254-3515-3

          2 3 4 5 Printing/Year 95 94 93 92 91

Printed in the United States of America

CONTENTS

Preface 7

Jacob's Ladder . . . A Way to God 9

Jacob . . . Who X-Rayed His Sons 14

The Hands of the Mighty God of Jacob 21

The Boy from the Country . . . Elisha 26

The Preacher Who Killed His Congregation 30

The Secret of Spiritual Blessedness 36

Happy Old Men 41

The Greatness of God 47

Blessed Are the Hungry! 56

Flies That Ruin the Ointment 60

God's Search for a Man 66

The Man with the Unwanted Tenant 70

The Best Place in the World 75

The Royal Wedding 81

Singing in the Rain 89

The Strange Commands of Jesus 98

When Christ Sat Down 106

Not Far From the Kingdom of God 112

Thou Shalt Call His Name—Jesus 118

A Reed Shaken by the Wind 123

God's Greatest Preacher 130

The People Who Desired to See Jesus 136

The Secrets of Christian Joy 143

The Bends in God's Roads 149

When Paul Made Up His Mind! 154

The Man Who Was Ready 160

Light at the End of a Tunnel 167

The Greatest Purchase Ever Made 172

The Magnificent Christ 180

Scripture Index 186

Bibliography 191

PREFACE

For several years, I have enjoyed the privilege of being one of the speakers at the Jubilee Meetings held in the Glen Haven Baptist Church, Decatur, Georgia. It was there I was first called *The Nugget Man.* At first, I was asked to deliver the message in services to which I had been assigned, but then, quite suddenly, an innovation occurred. When the interest appeared to be waning, or when spare time became available in the program, the pastor, without warning, would say: "Brother Ivor will give us one of his nuggets!" I was expected to speak from five to ten minutes, and in that brief period, a short story, an attractive outline, and a little humor supplied "sparkle" to the proceedings.

When preparing for these conferences I became accustomed to the task of "digging for nuggets" instead of formulating sermons. Year after year, I have recognized how my audiences appreciated those short stimulating messages. This book is the outcome of those Jubilee Meetings. I always prepare my notes in book form; each new discovery becomes a chapter, and their number is always increasing.

My friends will detect a change from the style of earlier volumes. Many young ministers asked if I would "put more flesh on the bones!" They liked my outlines but needed additional material to make sermon preparation easier. I have done as they requested.

Once again I express my thanks to Kregel Publications of Grand Rapids, Michigan. Their excellent work guarantees a wide circulation for my volumes. I consider the members of that family to be friends, and not merely my publishers. I am also indebted to the ministers whose constant encouragement made my writing worthwhile.

Bible Nuggets is affectionately dedicated to the Rev. Ralph Easterwood and his wonderful people in Decatur, Georgia. I shall always remember they were the first to call me "The Nugget Man."

Santa Barbara,   IVOR POWELL
California, 1991

Poor Jacob! He had become a wanderer far from home; he had stolen his brother's birthright; he had gained everything only to lose it again. Even the stars in the sky seemed unsympathetic. He had lost a mother; his father had been deceived; his brother Esau was outraged and threatening murder. Perhaps Jacob regretted his actions, but there was no possibility of turning back; he had, so to speak, burned his bridges! Somewhere beyond the horizon he might find people, but the prospect was not pleasing. A stranger in a foreign land would need friends, food, employment and a home in which to stay. The coveted birthright was poor compensation for the misery of his soul.

He was weary, every part of his body ached. His tired feet were burning from the long walk across the hot sands. Perhaps he found a small desert bush which offered shelter from the chilling winds, and, gathering stones as a pillow, the distracted man lay down to sleep, not caring if he would ever awaken. The poor fellow did not know Jehovah had watched every step he had taken that day, and even the angels were aware of his plight. "And he dreamed and behold a ladder set up on the earth, and the top of it reached to heaven. . . ."

The Ladder Was Surprising . . . *It led to God*

Anything Jacob knew about God was merely intellectual. His father and grandfather believed in Jehovah, and that knowledge had been shared with the fugitive. Yet he had never enjoyed fellowship with God, and he desired things which were prohibited. Doubtless, he was clever, shrewd and resourceful, but apart from personal pleasure, Jacob was another man destined to learn the hard way. It was therefore surprising when he discovered God had great interest in him, and had arranged something special to open his eyes. There was another world beyond human horizons where God reigned, and earthly treasures were unimportant. Jacob's ancestors had known about Jehovah, but apparently this was his first contact with the Almighty. He was still far short of what God required, and infinitely below what he might have been. Yet he would be unable

9

to deny the existence of Jehovah for he had heard His voice. The Lord had approached the runaway deceiver, and He was determined to change Jacob into the man he needed to become.

When Adam and Eve sinned in the garden of Eden, God sought them. Centuries later the Good Shepherd came to redeem undeserving people. God is always the Seeker; but it was significant that Jacob described the place as *dreadful*. Evidently he was uncomfortable in the presence of the Lord; much had to be accomplished within him.

The Ladder Was Sufficient . . . *It went all the way!*

". . . and the top of it reached to heaven." Obviously only God could provide such access into His presence. Earlier, when the inhabitants of earth spoke one language, the people decided they would bridge the gap between earth and heaven; between time and eternity. "And they said, Go to, let us build us a city, and a tower, whose top may reach unto heaven; and let us make us a name . . ." (Gen. 11:1-4). Those early builders had great ambitions but little intelligence. Apparently they disliked interference from heaven, and were determined to overthrow the authority of Jehovah. Their plans and ambitions were never completed, for God confounded the builders.

Many people in various ages tried to find a way into the presence of God, but their efforts always failed. Probably the most ardent were the Jews, who endeavored to create a religious and moral stairway to heaven. Their accomplishments always fell short of their need. John Bunyan described a man who entered the highway to heaven by climbing over a wall. The fellow avoided passing the Cross by taking a short cut into the highway of Grace. He appeared to be as safe as the Christian, for they traveled together. Unfortunately, his effort was insufficient to meet his need, for at the entrance to heaven he was rejected. His ladder was too short!

The Ladder Was Special . . . *It was the only one of its kind!*

Jacob never saw a second ladder; there was only one way into the Divine Presence. Centuries later, Jesus of Nazareth said to Nathaniel: "Because I said unto thee, I saw thee under the fig tree, believest thou? Thou shalt see greater things than these. And he saith unto him, Verily, verily, I say unto you, Hereafter ye shall see heaven open, and the angels of God ascending and descending upon the Son of Man" (John 1:50-51). Christ was the true Jacob's ladder, the means by which angels ascended and descended from heaven. Furthermore, He insisted that there was no other means of approaching God. He said: ". . . I am the way, the truth, and the life; *no man cometh unto the Father, but by me*" (John 14:6). Simon Peter preached identical truth when he said: "Neither is there salvation in any other: *for there is none other name under heaven given among men, whereby we must be saved*" (Acts 4:12). The Lord expressed the same truth when He said: "I am the door: by me if any man enter in, he shall be saved, and shall go in and out, and find pasture" (John 10:9). Sheepfolds had one door where the shepherd protected his flock.

During the history of the church, strange doctrines have been taught by opponents of the faith. It has been said that as there are twelve gates by which people enter the Holy City (Rev. 21:12), so there are many ways to come to God. The Hindus, the Moslems and other religions of the world have their idea of reaching the Hereafter, but as long as they reach their goal, it is unimportant how they get there. This is a contradiction of the teachings of Christ. The Savior insisted He was the only way by which to approach the Almighty. Many people dislike this interpretation, but it must be remembered: *Jesus taught this*; it is not a figment of human imagination. If unevangelized people of other nations safely reach an eternal home with God, why should the church spend incalculable wealth, time and energy taking the gospel message to those who have never heard? There is only one way to heaven, and people who travel by any other road will never reach their goal.

The Ladder Was Select . . . *It was used only by Angels!*

Jacob saw the ladder but never used it! Certain questions within his mind were answered during that memorable night, but one remained. He knew there was a God; that the Almighty ruled in heaven; that His promises made to the fathers were reliable. He realized that in spite of his indiscretions, the mercy of God was being extended in his direction. Yet, he did not know how *he could climb the ladder* into the presence of God. The dream indicated angels possessed a privilege denied to sinful men.

Many years later, Elijah appeared to have overcome that problem. "And it came to pass, as they still went on, and talked, that, behold, there appeared a chariot of fire, and horses of fire, and parted them both asunder; and Elijah went up by a whirlwind into heaven" (2 Kings 2:11). That was a definite improvement on what Jacob had seen earlier. To enter into the presence of God was now possible for God's servants. Unfortunately, Elijah had become a disappointment. His fear of Jezebel had undermined his faith in the preserving power of Jehovah. He could never again minister effectively to the people of Israel. The prophet did not climb a ladder; he was given a resplendent carriage in which to ride.

The Savior described how a beggar *"was carried by the angels into Abraham's bosom,"* whereas "the rich man also died, and was buried; And in hell, he lift up his eyes, being in torments, and seeth Abraham afar off, and Lazarus in his bosom" (Luke 16:22-23). It was remarkable that the beggar entered into eternal bliss, but the wealthy sinner did not. All these facts were extremely interesting, but they never answered the question—"How can sinners find the ladder, the chariot or any other transportation into the presence of God?"

That answer was supplied during the crucifixion of Jesus. Luke described how a guilty thief looked at Christ and prayed: "Lord, remember me when thou comest into thy kingdom. And Jesus said unto him, Verily, I say unto thee, Today shalt thou be with me in paradise" (Luke 23:42-43). The patriarch saw a ladder; the thief saw something more comprehensive. The cross pointed to heaven; reached down to earth; and two arms reached out to welcome everybody. Christ is all the human soul needs. To receive a visit from Him is to enjoy life's greatest privileges.

Miss Henderson was reading on the veranda of the Dufferin Hospital in India, when a high-class Hindu woman came up the steps to ask for an interview. As the missionary rose to welcome her, a copy of Holman Hunt's picture of Christ knocking upon a closed door fell out of her book. The visitor picked it up, and looking at it, said, "Tell me about this." Her request was granted and after hearing the gospel, the lady went away.

The following winter when snow was on the mountains, the missionary went to visit the woman. As she approached the house she saw the door was wide open, and the physical needs of the woman troubled her. She was a trained nurse, and said: "You should not have your door open. The mountains are covered with snow, and it is cold." The lady replied: "I know it. I have seen the snow, and have felt the cold, but I thought perhaps your Jesus might pass by, and I wanted Him to find the door wide open!" (Quoted from *One Hundred Great Texts and Their Treatment* by F. M. Barton, page 299).

Jacob was approaching death, and desiring to address his family for the last time, he summoned his children from their homes and estates. He sat in a chair beside his bed and surveyed the twelve sons who awaited his final statement. The aged father had much to say and was determined to be heard. With the eyes of a seer, he looked into the souls of his family, and sighed. Collectively, they were a disappointment but, among their number, one son at least shone as a brilliant star on a dark night. Many years later, David surveyed his army and came to an identical conclusion. Some of his soldiers were men of valor, but did not excel as did others. Theny were capable of leading small groups of men but would never qualify as generals. Centuries afterward, Christ addressed His followers who, like the sons of Jacob, were capable of being both delightful and difficult.

Reuben ... The Temperamental Man ... *Boiling!* (Gen. 49:3-4)

"Reuben, thou art my firstborn, my might, and the beginning of my strength, the excellency of dignity, and the excellency of power. *Unstable as water*, thou shalt not excel; because thou wentest up to thy father's bed; then defiledst thou it; he went up to my couch" (Gen. 49:3-4). The incident to which Jacob made reference is recorded in Genesis 35:22. "And it came to pass, when Israel dwelt in that land, that Reuben went and lay with Bilhah his father's concubine; and Israel heard it. ..." When the patriarch summed up the character of his firstborn, he said he was "*unstable as water*." Webster's Dictionary explains that the word means: "*Not fixed or steady; easily upset; changeable; fickle; emotionally unsettled.*" That definition revealed Jacob's thoughts concerning his eldest son. Water can boil and scald; become ice and freeze; it can be placid and unattractive; and also quench thirst and maintain life. It can be either helpful or harmful.

It was significant that Reuben was Jacob's "might, and the beginning of my strength, the excellency of dignity, and the excellency of power." He was handsome, dignified and very attractive. Perhaps that explains why Bilhah yielded to his persuasion and fell for a false lover. He might have been a leader in the nation; instead he was unimportant. When he "boiled" in his soul his outlook was distorted, and Reuben became the victim of his own passion. He was easily upset, and completely unreliable. Behind and beneath his dignified appearance was a slave to illegitimate desires.

Such people exist in every community. Talented men who would make excellent leaders lose their dignity and honor when, like Reuben, they permit evil to dominate their lives. Illicit attractions are too expensive to purchase! Some men and women cannot be trusted and are unfit for important assignments within the church. Their failure in moments of testing brings dishonor to the cause they represent.

Judah . . . The Tempestuous Man . . . *Belligerent*
(Gen. 49:8-10).

"Judah, thou art he whom thy brethren shall praise: *thine hand shall be in the neck of thine enemies*; thy father's children shall bow down before thee. *Judah is a lion's whelp: from the prey, my son, thou art gone up; he stooped down, he couched as a lion, and as an old lion*; who shall rouse him up? The sceptre shall not depart from Judah, nor a lawgiver from between his feet, until Shiloh come. . . ."

This man was a warrior; his descendants were the spearhead of Israel's military power. He was as a young lion roaming through a forest in search of prey, and as an older lion which, having devoured its victim, lies down to sleep. As a monarch he ruled the forest. Judah was a leader in his nation, but sometimes, people who love war never enjoy peace! The lust for domination and conquest becomes weakness when fighting is unjustified. Unlimited power makes a man indifferent to the pain of others. This was evident when Judah suggested selling his younger brother to strangers (Gen. 37:26-27). The ancient historian recorded one of the most disappointing episodes in Judah's life (Gen. 3).

Jacob's son had difficulty in admitting his errors; he hid them beneath the thin veneer of his self-righteousness. When he

15

was not fighting against other people, he was at war with himself. He would have been extremely uncomfortable had he listened to the words of Christ: "But I say unto you, Love your enemies, bless them that curse you, do good to them that hate you, and pray for them which despitefully use you, and persecute you" (Matt. 5:44).

Unfortunately, the descendants of Judah may be found in every church; they love to be leaders, and sometimes resent any challenge to their authority. They never make mistakes! Recognition of errors in other people is the fuel which feeds the fire of self-importance; they appear to be God-appointed rulers over all they survey. Prominent at church business meetings, they are very vocal when decisions have to be made concerning other people. As Jacob indicated, they will never change—until Shiloh come!

Zebulun . . . The Thoughtful Man . . . *Businesslike* (Gen. 49:13)

"Zebulun shall dwell at the haven of the sea; and he shall be for an haven of the ships; and his border shall be unto Zidon." The ancient boundaries of the tribe of Zebulun are somewhat obscure. The people had outlets to the sea and were interested in commerce and maritime trade. Practical people who were more interested in making money than in conquering their enemies, they supported their brothers in arms and possibly paid for their weapons, but continued trading. Other information concerning these businessmen is scarce, and it may be unwise to read into the text something not there!

It is safer to speak of this type of people who still exist within religious communities. No one could deny that the present generation resembles the tribes of Israel. Much remains to be accomplished before the church fully enters into her inheritance, but some are more interested in making money than in the conquest of the world for Christ. They give donations, but dislike being asked to be active in extending God's kingdom upon earth. Such people seldom pray unless their health and prosperity are threatened. They spend time with their financial reports but are too busy to read the scripture. Men may be

16

dying over the border, but nothing should be permitted to disturb the complacency of the man whose God is gold.

Issachar . . . The Tired Man . . . *Boring* (Gen. 49:14-15)

"Issachar is a strong ass couching (lying down) between two burdens: And he saw that rest was good, and the land that it was pleasant; and bowed his shoulders to bear, and became a servant unto tribute." The Berkley version of the scriptures offers the translation: "Issachar is a big-boned donkey, lying down between the sheep folds. When he finds rest enjoyable, and the land pleasant, he bends his shoulder to carry loads and submits to servitude."

Issachar is a donkey! Jacob's word-picture was enthralling. The bray of a donkey can be heard all over a village, but the animal seldom moves unless it is compelled to do so. This strange creature loves to lie down beside the tasks. He prefers the burden to be his pillow rather than a load on his back! The stupid animal responds more to kicks and curses than to entreaties. The ass seems to ask: "Who wants to work when God has given us sunshine? Work is for the unintelligent; rest should be endless!"

There are many donkeys within the church! They rejoice in the fact that God's love is like sunshine; they agree with everything taught, but they dislike work and responsibility. Labor is for other people. They prefer to supply lemonade to the workers than to roll up their sleeves! Donkeys have no enterprise, ambition or desire to work. They love to sleep. When the pastor preaches a stirring message about the joy of serving Christ, they open one eye, and close both ears. Their philosophy is simple — enough is enough! Even if it were possible, a donkey would never become a hunting dog or a racehorse. That would interfere with the sleeping schedule!

Dan . . . The Testy Man . . . *Biting* (Gen. 49:16-17)

Webster describes "testy" as being *easily irritated.* That explains why Jacob said: "Dan shall judge his people, as one of the tribes of Israel. *Dan shall be a serpent by the way, an adder in the path that biteth the horse heels*, so that his rider shall fall backward."

17

The adder to which the patriarch referred was the horned serpent which had the color of sand, and was marked with white and black spots. The reptile was exceptionally dangerous; its bite was fatal. It lay along the dusty roads where travelers were extremely careful. The snake was known to attack feet, and when a horse reared itself on its hind legs, riders were often thrown to become additional victims for the enemy in the sand. The statement probably referred to the instability of the tribesmen whose love for idols was notorious (Judges 18:27-31). The horned serpent was sly, patient and deadly, and, unfortunately, these characteristics were often seen among the Danites. They were sly; and they attacked from behind.

Probably Paul thought of such people when he wrote to the Romans and mentioned: "Backbiters, haters of God, despiteful, proud, boasters, inventors of evil things, disobedient to parents. . . . Who knowing the judgment of God, that they which commit such things are worthy of death, not only do the same, but have pleasure in them that do them" (Rom. 1:30-32). People who "bite behind the backs" of other people, have always been a menace within the church. Face-to-face confrontations provide hope of settling disputes, but those who whisper and circulate false allegations are a threat and should be avoided. One bite from that kind of snake can be fatal unless an antidote is applied quickly.

Asher . . . The Tasting Man . . . *Baking* (Gen. 49:20)

Evidently Jacob was not too impressed with his son Asher; what he had to say was expressed in fourteen words! Nevertheless the word picture given was extremely interesting. Asher was involved with lush pasture, excellent living, and a passion for "royal dainties"! Jacob said: "*Out of Asher his bread shall be fat, and he shall yield royal dainties.*" When the land of Canaan was divided among the tribes, Asher was given the strip of coastland north of Mount Carmel. It was exceedingly fertile and included some of the best orchards and olive groves in the country. No outstanding military leader came from its people, and prosperity made it selfish and independent. "His bread shall be fat" could suggest over-indulgence, but the next statement provides food for thought. It would be interesting to know more about "the royal dainties." Were these provided exclusively for the king? Does the statement imply that Asher specialized in the creating, or obtaining of delicacies? Would they pay and do anything to obtain things which made them fat?

That interpretation may not be justified, but the type of people described can be found in every church. They are the over-fed Christians who need exercise rather than a sumptuous meal, and are called "sermon-tasters." These folk develop a passion for the sweet things of life and dislike what is needed. They go from church to church listening to different speakers; and comparing one with another, they often fail to hear the voice of God. In this respect they are like the tribe of Naphthali of whom Jacob said: "*Napthali is a hind let loose: he giveth goodly words.*" A hind or deer roams over great distances; is hard to find; feeds on varying pastures, and is easily shot! Every pastor is aware of the members who go from one feeding place to another. They are hard to locate, and are often wounded by hunters. The sons of Jacob have lived a long time!

Joseph . . . The Thrilling Man . . . *Blessing* (Gen. 49:22-26)

"*Joseph is a fruitful bough, even a fruitful bough by a well; whose branches run over the wall.*" There is a vast difference between a tree planted by a well, and one struggling to survive in the desert. Moisture is indispensable for good growth, but Jacob knew his favorite son was nourished by the unfailing supplies of divine grace. This had always been evident. God overruled the cruelty of his brethren; the lies told in Egypt; the unwarranted imprisonment and subsequent rise to national prominence. It was impossible for bitterness to reside in a forgiving soul, and revenge could not exist within a gracious spirit. Joseph drew his daily supplies from the wells of God's salvation, and as a result "his branches (daughters) ran over the wall." The man's influence had spread beyond the normal outreach of ordinary people; his fame was unprecedented.

There appeared to be no limit to the things God would do for

His servant. "Even by the God of thy father, who shall help thee; and by the Almighty, who shall bless thee with blessings of heaven above; blessings of the deep that lieth under; blessings of the breasts, and of the womb . . ." (Gen. 49:25).

This remarkable text not only summarized the life of Joseph; it explained the secret of his success. (1) *He was special* — "a fruitful bough"; (2) *He was sustained* — "by a well"; (3) *He was successful* — "whose branches run over the wall"; (4) *He was safe* — "made strong by the mighty hands of the God of Jacob."

Blessed is the pastor whose congregation includes people like Joseph. It would be impossible to calculate their value to the church of God. It might be refreshing for everybody to ask:

> What kind of a church would my church be
> If every member were just like me?

THE HANDS OF THE MIGHTY GOD OF JACOB
(GENESIS 49:22-24)

The imagery in this scripture is very suggestive, for the aged Jacob, in blessing his sons, saw Joseph as a fruitful tree planted by a well. Drawing sustenance from the depths of God's grace, Joseph had become prosperous in many ways, and his influence had spread over the walls which protected the grove. Jacob's favorite son had been used by God in Egypt, and from the heavenly source had come—or would come—*"The Shepherd or Rock of Israel."* Many commentators believe this to be a Messianic prediction fulfilled when the hands of Jesus supplied healing to suffering people.

Rescuing Peter from Drowning . . . *How Strong* (Matt. 14:30-31)

"But when he (Peter) saw the wind boisterous, he was afraid; and beginning to sink, he cried, saying, Lord, save me. And immediately *Jesus stretched forth his hand*, and caught him, and said unto him, O thou of little faith, wherefore didst thou doubt?" Perhaps Peter's response to the invitation of the Lord was impulsive and irrational, but his faith was commendable. He walked upon the water and did the apparently impossible. It should always be remembered that as long as he looked at the Lord, *he did not sink!* Christ imparted to His follower something which He alone possessed. Furthermore, when Peter's faith diminished and he cried for help, Jesus did what no other person could have done. To lift a drowning man, the rescuer must be standing on something solid — otherwise, the desperate man will pull him down. Peter's experience was an example of Christ's strength being made perfect in the disciple's weakness (2 Cor. 12:9).

The Savior's attitude toward Simon Peter may be summarized under four headings. He *loved; looked; listened* and *lifted*. It is encouraging to know that Christ remains the unchanging One. "Jesus Christ the same yesterday, and today, and for ever" (Heb. 13:8). Life is filled with storms which can be more threatening than any which disturbed the Sea of Galilee. Problems ruin serenity, but in every emergency the Lord is able and willing to help those who call upon Him.

Reclaiming the Leper from Despair . . . *How Suggestive*
    (Matt. 8:2-3)

"And, behold, there came a leper and worshipped him, saying, Lord, if thou wilt, thou canst make me clean. *And Jesus put forth his hand* and touched him, saying, I will; be thou clean. And immediately his leprosy was cleansed." It was illegal for any leper to approach other people. Lepers were isolated, for there was always danger of contagion. It may never be known how fierce was the conflict within the mind of the sufferer who came to Christ. If he disobeyed the law, he could be stoned. Probably he knew death was inevitable whatever he did. If he did nothing the disease would kill him; if he went to Jesus and was arrested, his premature death would be a welcome release from suffering. There appeared to be some hope at the feet of the Savior and any risk involved was worth taking. Nevertheless, the leper never expected Christ to touch him. That action was considered beyond the realm of possibility, for to touch a leper was not only dangerous; it was defiling. Evidently God's power met the man's need where it was. The Lord was above the law and everything that accompanied it. It was significant that throughout His ministry, no person ever came in vain to Jesus. Once again the incident may be summarized under four headings—*The law with its prohibition* (see Leviticus 14). *The leper with his problem. The Lord with His power. The liberation with its praise.*

Restoring the Beggar from Darkness . . . *How Sufficient*
    (Mark 8:22-25)

"And he cometh to Bethsaida; and they bring a blind man unto him, and besought him to touch him. And he took the blind man by the hand, and led him out of the town; and when he had spit on his eyes, *and put his hands upon him,* he asked if he saw ought. And he looked up and said, I see men as trees, walking. After that *he put his hands again upon his eyes*, and made him look up: and he was restored, and saw every man clearly."

This was a remarkable account, for it revealed facets of Christ's ministry not mentioned elsewhere. The fact that this man was brought to Jesus indicated friends cared about his condition. Throughout the history of the church theologians debated the reason for the gradual recovery of this man's sight. Could not Christ have completed the miracle instantly? The Savior decided it would be better to heal the man by stages. For this there could be several reasons. Perhaps the man's health necessitated a gradual improvement. The sudden inrush of light might have caused other physical damage. The Pulpit Commentary interprets the passage as: "I see men; for I behold them as trees walking; that is, I see something confusedly and obscurely; not clearly, for I see what I think must be men, and yet so dimly that they look to me like trees only that I know men move from their places, whereas trees do not" (*Pulpit Commentary*. "Mark," pg. 333). Perhaps Christ rewarded the man according to his faith. An imperfect faith was answered by an incomplete miracle. Christ encouraged the beggar to "believe with all his heart" that even greater things could be performed on his behalf. Jesus demonstrated the fact that He was able to meet the man's need under all circumstances, and what He did then, He still performs for all who trust Him.

Relieving the Widow from Difficulty . . . *How Splendid* (Luke 13:11-13)

"And, behold, there was a woman which had a spirit of infirmity eighteen years, and was bowed together, and could in no wise lift up herself. And when Jesus saw her, he called her to him, and said unto her, Woman, thou art loosed from thine infirmity. *And he laid his hands on her*, and immediately she was made straight, and glorified God." The age of this afflicted woman is not known, but she had probably spent half of her life as a victim of a crippling disease. She was troubled by a malady which affected her spine, and consequently could not even lift her head to see the Savior. When Jesus called her, even though she could not see Him, at least she heard His voice — and obeyed! That was the secret of the transformation which removed her disability.

There are innumerable people whose sight is limited; oppressive circumstances prevent their recognition of the goodness of God. The Lord never asks the impossible. When men are overwhelmed by problems, God calls, and obedience makes all things possible. There was no religious order which could perform miracles; the secret of recovery was in a personal confrontation with the living Christ, and as it was long ago, it remains unchanged today.

Releasing the Disciples from Doubt . . . *How Safe* (John 10:27-29)

"My sheep hear my voice, and I know them, and they follow me. And I give unto them eternal life, and they shall never perish, neither shall any man pluck them *out of my hand.* My Father which gave them me, is greater than all, and no man is able to pluck them *out of my Father's hand.*" The "double-grip" of the hands of The Father and Son provides immeasurable strength and incomparable safety. This is a delightful endorsement of the words spoken by Jacob. ". . . the arms of his hands were made strong by the hands of the mighty God of Jacob — from thence is the shepherd, the stone of Israel" (Gen. 49:24).

Jesus realized the future of His followers would be hazardous; Simon Peter would be ashamed of his inconsistency; Thomas worried by his doubts, and others a prey to their fear. After each failure, despondency would harass the minds of His dearest friends, and the thought of being unworthy of God's kindness could haunt them throughout their earthly pilgrimage. The Lord was emphatic when He announced that nothing would be able to pluck them from "the double-grip" of the divine Family. Paul evidently believed this fact, for he wrote: "For I am persuaded, that neither death, nor life, nor angels, nor principalities, nor powers, nor things present, nor things to come, Nor height, nor depth, nor any other creature, shall be able to separate us from the love of God, which is in Christ Jesus our Lord" (Rom. 8:38-39).

The keeping power of God's hand is sufficient for every emergency of life. It was written that the Lord Jesus "took them (little children) up into his arms, put his hands upon them, and blessed them" (Mark 10:16). At the other extreme of life, David said: "Whither shall I go from thy spirit? or whither shall I flee from thy presence? If I ascend up into heaven, thou art there: if I make my bed in hell, behold, thou art there. If I take the wings of the morning and dwell in the uttermost parts of the sea; Even there shall thy hand lead me, and thy right hand shall hold me" (Ps. 139:7-10).

THE BOY FROM THE COUNTRY ... Elisha
(1 KINGS 19:19, JOHN 7:39)

One of the most respected citizens in a small town in York-shire, England, was both the police officer and the veterinarian. When his wife answered the telephone one evening, a lady asked if her husband were at home. "In what capacity do you need him?" inquired the lady of the house. "Well," came the reply, "I need him both as a vet and as a policeman. I cannot get my bulldog to open his mouth—and there is a burglar inside it!" That simple story explains my task. I have a strange verse. If I can open it, there is treasure inside!

The Call in the Country ... *A Decision to Follow*

It was probably a delightful morning when Elisha took his oxen to plow in the field. He could not have known it was to be his last day on the farm; his life was about to be transformed. He was like any other farmer in the area and fervently desired to be successful. Evidently he had partially reached that goal, for he owned his equipment, and twenty-four sturdy oxen. During the morning he saw a stranger approaching, and was astonished when a cloak was thrown over his head and shoulders. Elisha had heard of Elijah the prophet, for the entire nation was aware of the confrontation which had occurred on Mount Carmel, and the anger of Jezebel when she heard of the assassination of her priests. Yet, in all probability, the plowman had no previous contact with the man of God.

It was significant that God's call never went to a student nor teacher in one of the schools of the prophets. Elijah did not solicit the services of a nobleman's son, he went to a farmer. It is also interesting that Elisha was not influenced by Elijah's failure, nor the possibility of financial loss if he accepted a call to the ministry. He slew a yoke of oxen and distributed the meat among neighbors. The plow was destroyed and used as firewood. The other oxen were probably given to his family or friends, and it became evident there was never a possibility he would regret or renounce his commitment. The decision to follow Elijah was the commencement of a remarkable ministry.

Many years later, another Teacher walked through Palestine. He met fishermen at their boats, a tax-gatherer at his place of business, and other people with ordinary occupations. He never called a college graduate nor professional of any kind. He, so to speak, threw His mantle over poor men whose hands were calloused from earning a living. It was significant that the original apostles never returned to their former occupations during the ministry of their Master. As they commenced their new career, they "burned their bridges behind them." Having placed their hands upon the plow, they never looked back!

The Concern of the Convert . . . *A Desire to Feel!*

"Then he (Elisha) arose and went after Elijah, and ministered unto him" (1 Kings 19:21). He did not perform miracles, nor accomplish anything sensational, but he was completely dependable. He was always present when Elijah required assistance; nothing could entice him from his place of service. Maybe he prepared meals and provided fellowship, which was always an antidote for loneliness. Yet, the more he served Elijah, the greater became his concern. He knew his master possessed unusual qualities which he did not have. One day when Elijah said: "Ask what I shall do for thee, before I be taken away from thee," Elisha responded: "I pray thee, let a double portion of thy spirit be upon me" (2 Kings 2:9). Because he was acutely aware of his insufficiency, Elisha yearned to be more like his master.

Centuries later the disciples of Christ reached the same conclusion. They followed Jesus, saw His mighty deeds, and even tried to emulate His example, but their best efforts fell short of what they desired. This became evident when a troubled father sought deliverance for a tormented son (Matt. 17:19). Their problem was accentuated when, like Elijah, the Savior announced His imminent departure. They would be confronted by insurmountable obstacles, and evidently needed a double portion of the Holy Spirit. The Lord said: ". . . he that believeth on me, the works that I do shall he do also; *and greater works than these shall* he do; because I go unto my Father . . . And I will pray the Father, and he shall give you another Comforter, that he may

27

abide with you for ever" (John 14:12, 16, italics mine). Elisha was a window through which it was easy to see the church.

The Challenge of the Commission . . . *A Direction to Fulfill*

Things which are obtained easily are often of no value. Eternal life is a gift from God, but the price to be paid for the fulness of the Holy Spirit demands more than some people are willing to pay. Elijah's response to his servant's petition was clear and concise. He said: "Thou hast asked a hard thing: nevertheless if thou see me when I am taken from thee, it shall be so unto thee; but if not, it shall not be so" (2 Kings 2:10). Evidently Elisha had to be faithful to the end, but that presented problems. Elijah had established colleges at Bethel and Jericho where young men were trained for the ministry, and at both these centers attractive proposals were made to Elijah's servant. He could have become a popular teacher, for his knowledge of the great Elijah would have made him a competent professor. He might have become the president of an institution. His services would have been in great demand, and his engagements exceedingly lucrative. The refusal to accept the invitations revealed the resolution of his soul. He had determined to stay with Elijah, and that was exactly what he did.

Many of the people who heard the Savior's final words were not as wise. Paul indicated the risen Christ "was seen of above five hundred brethren at once . . ." (1 Cor. 15:6). Probably that referred to the time when the Lord ascended into the presence of His Father. "And being assembled together with them, he commanded them that they should not depart from Jerusalem, but wait for the promise of the Father, which, saith he, ye have heard of me . . . ye shall receive power, after that the Holy Ghost is come upon you . . ." (Acts 1:4 and 8). More than 500 people heard those words, but it remains a mystery why, for reasons unknown, 380 never stayed long enough to enjoy the thrill of Pentecost. What happened to them?

The Conquests of the Consecrated . . . *A Description of Faithfulness*

Elisha requested a *double* portion of his master's spirit, and

28

it was significant that he performed *twice as many miracles* as Elijah did. Furthermore, if he may be judged by his deeds, he was the most Christlike of all the prophets. For example, after he was filled with the Holy Spirit, he raised the dead (2 Kings 4:19-36 and Luke 7:15); fed hungry people (2 Kings 4:42-44 and Matt. 15:32-39); cleansed a leper (2 Kings 5:10-14 and Matt. 16:9-10); and gave sight to the blind (2 Kings 6:20 and Luke 18:35-43). Finally, life was given through his death (2 Kings 13:20-21 and John 3:16).

It is important to know the prelude to these marvelous experiences. The type suggests the servant "died" with his master. Elijah and Elisha went through Jordan together (Rom. 6:6). When Christ died, our carnal nature was reckoned as crucified with the Redeemer. Yet, that was not enough to guarantee the fulness of divine blessing. After Elisha destroyed his own garments — that is, after he renounced his self-life, he put on the mantle of Elijah and returned to the same river to cross it alone (Gal. 2:20). Likewise Paul also claimed that he passed through his Jordan—his Calvary—daily (see 1 Cor. 15:31). It was continuous identification with Christ in death which led to the success of the apostle's evangelistic crusades. He and Elisha proved the truth of the Scripture: ". . . Not by might, nor by power, but by my spirit, saith the LORD of hosts" (Zech. 4:6).

Many years ago, J. Allen Tupper and a friend were being escorted around the interesting barracks at Fort Monroe. The guide pointed to a large gun and exclaimed: "With that gun we could pulverise great stone walls, and kill many enemies thousands of yards away." The friend replied: "That is not so; the gun by itself is useless." "Oh," said the officer, "of course we must first insert the powder and shell, and then the disastrous work will begin." The friend replied: "Even that is not enough. You still need the spark which will send the shell toward its target." The Rev. Tupper said: "We may have big guns in the pulpit, and possess the finest equipment, but unless we have the fire of the Holy Spirit, we shall never shatter the strongholds of Satan, nor bring in the reign of our spiritual King."

THE PREACHER WHO KILLED
HIS CONGREGATION (2 Chronicles 13:18)

Hidden among the historical events of antiquity is a story of a young king whose faith shone as a beacon in the darkness. It describes how on the eve of a great battle he preached an eloquent sermon, but unfortunately, listeners refused to heed his advice, and their folly was fatal.

After the death of Solomon, the nation of Israel was divided and continuing antagonism led to a civil war. Jeroboam, a mighty man of valor, had been crowned by ten tribes, and Abijah, who succeeded Rehoboam, reigned over Judah. The respective armies were ready for combat when a surprising event took place. Josephus, the famous historian, described the scene.

"Now, as the armies stood in array, ready for action and dangers, Abijah stood upon an elevated place, and, beckoning with his hand, he desired the multitude and Jeroboam himself to hear first with silence what he had to say. And when silence was made, he began to speak, and told them: 'God had consented that David and his posterity should be their rulers for all time to come, and this, you yourselves are not unacquainted with; but I cannot but wonder how you should forsake my father, and join yourselves to his servant Jeroboam, and are now here with him to fight against those, who by God's determination, are to reign . . . but you considered nothing of all this. And what is it you depend upon for victory! Is it upon those golden heifers and the altars that you have on high places which are demonstrations of your impiety, and not of religious worship? Or is it the exceeding multitude of your army which gives you such good hopes? Yet certainly there is no strength at all in an army of many ten thousands when the war is unjust, for we ought to place our surest hopes of success against our enemies in righteousness alone, and in piety towards God; which hope we justly have, since we have kept the laws from the beginning, and have worshipped our own God, who was not made by hands out of corruptible matter, nor was He formed by a wicked king, in order to deceive the multitude; but who is His own workmanship, and the beginning and end of all things. I therefore even now give you counsel to repent, and to take better advice, and to leave off the prosecution of the war, to call to mind the laws of your country and to reflect what it hath been that hath advanced you to so happy a state as ye are now in.'

"This was the speech which Abijah made to the multitude. But while he was still speaking, Jeroboam sent some of his soldiers privately to encompass Abijah round about on certain parts of the camp that were not taken notice of . . ." (*The Works of Flavius Josephus*, Book 8, Chapter 11, Paragraphs 2-3).

It is not difficult to visualize that young king speaking from his elevated position to the multitude across the valley. His faith in God was almost beyond comprehension. The incident may be considered under three headings.

The Terrible Predicament . . . *How Frightening*

He was outclassed. Jeroboam, the rebel leader, was an expert at making war. The ancient writer said of him: "And the man Jeroboam was a mighty man of valour: and Solomon seeing the young man was industrious, he made him ruler over all the charge of the house of Joseph" (1 Kings 11:28). The prowess and courage of this captain was known throughout the nation, and after the king, Rehoboam, failed to alleviate the sufferings of the common people, the discontented tribes asked him to champion their cause. When Abijah became king of Judah, he had little if any military experience, and it became evident he was wearing a crown too heavy for comfort. It is said that "Jeroboam despised him for his youth," but the new monarch did not avoid his responsibilities. He gathered an army, and with great faith in God and his cause, went to the battle. He would have appreciated the words of Paul: "What shall we then say to these things? If God be for us, who can be against us?" (Rom. 8:31).

He was outnumbered. "And Abijah set the battle in array with an army of valiant men of war, even four hundred thousand chosen men: Jeroboam also set the battle in array against him with eight hundred thousand chosen men, being mighty men of valour" (2 Kings 13:3). Some theologians dispute the accuracy of these numbers, believing the opposing armies were smaller. Josephus agreed that the army of Abjiah was four hundred thousand, "but the army of Jeroboam *was double to it.*" The important detail of the story is that the Israelites enjoyed an advantage of two-to-one over Judah, and that, under any circumstance, would have been formidable. Evidently, Abijah believed God was the God of minorities and shared the conviction expressed by the two spies who assured Moses it was possible to overcome the inhabitants of the promised land (Num. 14:6-9). Men and women of faith never lose sight of God. Even David said to Goliath: ". . . Thou comest to me with a sword, and with a spear and with a shield: but I come to thee in the name of the LORD of hosts, the God of the armies of Israel, whom thou hast defied. This day will the LORD deliver thee into mine hand . . ." (1 Sam. 17:45-46). David was only a youth, but he was tall enough to look beyond Goliath and see Jehovah.

He was outmaneuvered. "But Jeroboam caused an ambushment to come about behind them: so they were before Judah, and the ambushment was behind them. And when Judah looked back, behold, the battle was before and behind: and they cried unto the Lord, and the priests sounded with the trumpets. Then the men of Judah gave a shout: and as the men of Judah shouted, it came to pass, that God smote Jeroboam and all Israel before Abijah and Judah" (2 Chron. 13:13-15). As Josephus indicated, the treachery of Jeroboam was unmistakable in that he used the speech as a cover for clandestine operations.

Evidently there was a nearby hill or gully by which some of the soldiers of Jeroboam reached the rear of Abijah's army, and when the men of Judah were fighting for their lives, a wave of fresh attackers came behind them, and it seemed the beseiged men would either die or be compelled to surrender. The men of Judah had been outwitted by a merciless enemy who failed to understand that God could not be ambushed! When the great battles of life are fought, it helps to have God on your side!

The historian described how, in their extremity, the men of Judah (a) *cried unto the Lord*; (b) *the priests sounded with their trumpets*; and (c) *the entire army shouted with a great shout.* ". . . and as the men of Judah shouted, it came to pass that God

smote Jeroboam and all Israel before Abijah and Judah. . . .
And Abijah and his people slew them with a great slaughter: so
there fell down slain of Israel five hundred thousand chosen
men" (2 Chron. 13:15-17).

Much might be said of the king's emotional appeal, but in
the final analysis, more must be said of the mercy of God.
Although they did not realize the importance of the occasion, a
half a million souls were receiving Jehovah's final warning.
The incident teaches (1) *How important is God's message*; (2)
How inspiring is God's mercy; (3) *How imposing is God's
majesty*. There is always a way of escape for sinners, but when
they refuse to accept it, punishment is inevitable.

The Tremendous Preaching . . . *How Faithful*

Probably this was one of the greatest Old Testament sermons ever preached. Its theme, its content and the power with
which it was delivered, suggest the preacher would have been a
worthy companion for Simon Peter and Paul.

It was fearless. The speaker had no intention of "playing to
the gallery!" He accused his opponent of betraying everything
decent and sacred, and his remarks were directed personally
toward the person most concerned. Evidently, he expressed the
thoughts which occupied his mind. If at a later time he were
required to answer for his verbal abuse, he would bravely confront his demise. Yet, even in death, he would know he had
spoken truth, and not compromised his convictions.

It was factual. Israel's difficulties had been increased by
national decadence. The tribes had forsaken God and their "old-
time religion"; the faith of their fathers had been sacrificed
upon strange altars. The king's sermon was comprehensive in
that it covered many areas.

The people had *no excuse*, for the tribes had been defiant in
their rebellion. They had *no sanctuary*. They had deserted the
temple in Jerusalem, and erected substitutes in Bethel and Dan.
This was a revival of the pre-Abrahamic bull worship condemned by God and His servants. The nation had *no priest*.
Jeroboam's false ministers offered incantations and sacrifices
before their idols, but they had no contact with Jehovah. They

had *no Savior*. The confidence of the people had been placed in golden calves, as was the case when Moses received the commandments on Mount Sinai. Israel had *no conscience*. When they listened to the voice of the royal evangelist, they heard nothing! When the call to repentance was made, they were already planning to outwit their opponents. They were beyond redemption.

They had *no hope*. They were dead even before they died! It was remarkable that an ancient speaker who never attended any school of the prophets, should become such a dynamic evangelist. He was more proficient in his mountain pulpit than he was in his palace. Evidently, he believed in the Psalmist's theology: "Happy is that people, whose God is the LORD" (Ps. 144:15). That he preached in vain proved the decadence of the nation. Unfortunately, revolution was more popular than revival, and that unfortunate situation led to tragedy.

The Thrilling Preservation . . . *How fabulous*

". . . and the children of Judah prevailed, *because they relied upon the LORD God of their fathers*." This was one of the most conclusive battles in the long and troubled history of the nation. Palestine was not a large country, and since the defeated ten tribes lost half a million chosen men, Israel not only suffered a humiliating defeat; the fathers of that generation were annihilated leaving only children and aging men. That explained the complete inability of the vanquished people to recruit another army during the reign of Abijah. "Neither did Jeroboam recover strength again in the days of Abijah." It is interesting that the historian was more concerned with how the battle was won than in the magnificence of the military achievement. He mentioned four features which invite examination.

Their Problem. *". . . the battle was before and behind . . ."*

The young king was unaware of the treachery of his opponent, and was devastatingly surprised when, in the heat of the battle, a new army attacked from the rear. Undoubtedly, confusion overwhelmed the soldiers of Judah who, for a few threatening moments, hardly knew what to do.

Their Prayer. *". . . and they cried unto the Lord . . ."*

That was possibly the greatest prayer meeting ever assembled. Men fought for their lives, and at the same time asked God to intervene. That was at least one occasion when men prayed with their eyes open! The incident provided a classic example of the doctrine of James who said: "Faith without works is dead" (James 2:20). When all else fails, it pays to pray.

Their Praise. *". . . and the priests sounded with the trumpets"*

The electrifying notes of the trumpets, heard above the noise of combat, revived and renewed the strength of the men of Judah, who, with increasing confidence and zeal, attacked their startled enemies. Centuries later the Savior said to His disciples: ". . . What things soever ye desire, when ye pray, *believe that ye receive them*, and ye shall have them" (Mark 11:24). Faith is a much stronger weapon than anything manufactured by men.

Their Partner. *"God smote Jeroboam and all Israel"*

It was never revealed how God destroyed the people who refused to obey His commandments. He overwhelmed the Egyptians by permitting towering walls of water to collapse on their pursuing army (Exod. 14:26-27). He defeated the host of the Syrians by allowing them to hear the movements of a heavenly host (2 Kings 7:6-7). The Lord destroyed a host of Philistines during a terrific thunderstorm, when, in all probability lightning caused havoc among the soldiers (1 Sam. 7:10). God has innumerable weapons in His arsenal, but faith is the key which unlocks the storehouse of heaven's resources. Blessed is the man who knows he is never alone. Throughout their acute danger, the men of Judah relied completely upon God, and that was the secret of their invincibility. God has never changed. The writer to the Hebrews knew this for he wrote: "Jesus Christ the same yesterday, and to day, and for ever" (Heb. 13:8).

THE SOURCE AND SECRET OF
SPIRITUAL BLESSEDNESS (PSALM 1:1-3)

There is a vast difference between a petrified forest and trees bearing fruit in an orchard! The one is a memorial to an ancient tragedy when life terminated. The other is a reminder that care and nourishment can overcome challenges to existence. The first time I saw a petrified forest I shuddered, for the wood had become stone. It was written of Nabal that when Abigail informed him of David's anger, "his heart died within him, and he became as a stone" (1 Sam. 25:37).

As a contrast, the Psalmist described a devout man as "a tree planted by the rivers of water, that bringeth forth his fruit in his season; his leaf also shall not wither, and whatsoever he doeth shall prosper." Such a tree suggests *roots, response, refreshments* and *rewards*. Blessed is the tree (man) whose roots go deep into righteousness; which responds to care; drinks freely from eternal supplies, and fulfills the intention of its owner. Such human trees cannot live in vain, nor cease to exist. They perpetuate themselves in others who emulate their example. The Bible explains the success of all people planted close to God's river of life.

Trees full of sap . . . *The Suggestive Statement*

"The trees of the LORD are full of sap; the cedars of Lebanon, which he hath planted; Where the birds make their nests; as for the stork, the fir trees are her house" (Ps. 104:16-17). Charles Haddon Spurgeon wrote: "The trees uncared for by man are yet so full of sap, we may rest assured that the people of God who by faith live upon the Lord alone, shall be equally well sustained. Planted by grace, and owing all to our heavenly Father's care, we may defy the hurricane, and laugh at the fear of drought, for none that trust in Him shall ever be unwatered." He also wrote: "The transition which the Psalmist makes from men to trees is as if he had said: 'It is not to be wondered at if God so bountifully nourishes men, who are created after His own image, He does not grudge to extend His care even to trees. By *the trees of the Lord* is meant those which are high and of

36

surpassing beauty; for God's blessings are more conspicuous in them. It seems scarcely possible for any juice of the earth to reach so great a height, and yet they renew their foliage every year (John Calvin).'" Both quotations are from *The Treasury of David*, pg. 434, published by Kregel Publications, Grand Rapids, Michigan.

It must be remembered this statement refers to "The trees of THE LORD." God was the first either to create or plant trees; there is no ancient reference to men planting forests. Perhaps David had three thoughts in mind when he referred to "*trees planted by the rivers of water.*" (1) *Desire.* He knew the value of healthy trees; they could provide shade from the sun; homes for the birds; beauty for the landscape, and often, fruit for the hungry. (2) *Design.* He placed them by rivers that they could be nourished in times of drought. (3) *Delight.* God desired His world to be beautiful. It could exist without flowers and trees, but their presence indicated God provided everything necessary for the happiness of His people. That He likened men to trees planted by the rivers of water signifies the same things. The Lord desired humans to be sources of blessing to all people, and to make this possible, arranged that spiritual nourishment would always be available. "*Trees full of sap*" suggests dedicated men, filled with the Holy Spirit, giving to the world what it so urgently needs.

Clouds full of rain . . . *The Significant Source*

"If the clouds be *full of rain*, they empty themselves upon the earth . . ." (Eccl. 11:3). Perhaps, this should be the first text to consider, for "All good gifts around us are sent from heaven above." Without rain a beautiful garden may become a wilderness. Unless moisture falls from the sky, landscapes resemble a desert. It was significant that Solomon said: ". . . and if a tree fall toward the south, or toward the north, in the place where the tree falleth, there it shall be" (Eccl. 11:3). It appeared he was referring to irrefutable laws prevailing in the universe. Clouds filled with rain would inevitably drop moisture, and trees uprooted by a storm would fall either in one direction or another, and therefore would remain motionless. The same fact prevails within the spiritual realm. Unless rain fell from heaven, rivers would never be filled with water, and crops could not be harvested. When Elijah's prayers closed the heavens for three and a half years, all rivers in Israel ceased to flow, and water holes dried up. Cattle died; crops were destroyed and people became hungry. Later when the nation repented of sin, Elijah prayed again, and ". . . the heaven was black with clouds and wind, and there was a great rain" (1 Kings 18:45). The greatest skills of man cannot be an effective substitute for God's blessings. When deprived of divine enabling. men become motionless machinery. David realized this fact when he wrote: "I will lift up mine eyes unto the hills, from whence cometh my help. My help cometh from the LORD, which made heaven and earth" (Ps. 121:1-2).

A river full of water . . . *The Sufficient Supply*

"Thou visitest the earth, and waterest it: thou greatly enrichest it with the river of God, which is full of water . . ." (Ps. 65:9). Evidently the Psalmist believed Jehovah was the Sustainer of the entire earth. He wrote: "Thou waterest the ridges thereof abundantly; thou settlest the furrows thereof; thou makest it soft with showers: thou blessest the springing thereof. Thou crownest the year with thy goodness; and thy paths drop fatness" (Ps. 65:10-11). It is thought-provoking to discover the Bible has much to say about the river of God. Ezekiel described two rivers which came from beneath the altar. He said: "Now when I had returned, behold, at the bank of the river were very many trees on the one side and on the other. Then said he unto me, These waters issue out toward the east country, and go down into the desert, and go into the sea; which being brought forth into the sea, the waters shall be healed. And it shall come to pass . . . *everything shall live whither the river cometh*" (Ezek. 47:7-9). John wrote: "And he shewed me a pure river of water of life, clear as crystal, proceeding out of the throne of God and the Lamb. In the midst of the street of it, and on either side of the river, was there the tree of life, which bare twelve manner of fruits, and yielded her fruit every month: and the leaves of the tree were for the healing of the nations" (Rev.

22:1-2). David also wrote: "There is a river, the streams whereof shall make glad the city of God, the holy place of the tabernacles of the most High" (Ps. 46:4). *The rivers of God are always full!* It is interesting that, having referred to the *river of God*, the Psalmist then spoke of the streams which would make glad the inhabitants of the city of God. As tributaries supply water to the river, so the river supplies many irrigation ditches. This adds importance to other texts which describe the enrichment of those who drink God's living water.

Micah said: "But truly I am *full of power* by the Spirit of the LORD . . ." (3:8). The Amplified Version describes Stephen as being *full of grace*. "Now Stephen full of grace—(divine blessing and favor) worked great wonders and signs—(miracles) among the people" (Acts 6:8). Deuteronomy describes Joshua as being "*full of the spirit of wisdom*." The high priest of Israel was required to have hands "*full of sweet incense*." His approach to the altar on the day of atonement could be recognized by the perfume of the incense; he was to be holy in the sight of God. Jesus mentioned the *fullness of joy* which He desired His followers to know. "These things have I spoken unto you, that my joy might remain in you, and your *your joy might be full*" (John 15:11). God's grace is sufficient to meet the needs of His children. There would never be any impoverished believers if the followers of Christ drank freely from God's everlasting supplies.

Floors full of wheat . . . *The Special Success*

"Be glad then, ye children of Zion, and rejoice in the LORD your God: for he hath given you the former rain and the latter rain in the first month. And *the floors (threshing floors) shall be full of wheat*, and the fats (vats) shall overflow with wine (grape juice) and oil" (Joel 2:23-24, *Amplified Version*). The writings of this prophet predicted future events, but the truth enshrined in his book applied to all ages. When God's people availed themselves of God's provision, the result was assured. Jehovah's unfailing supplies would guarantee harvests of every kind. Joel wrote: "And ye shall eat in plenty, and be satisfied, and praise the name of the LORD your God, that hath dealt wondrously with you: and my people shall never be ashamed. And ye shall know that I am in the midst of Israel, and that I am the LORD your God, and none else: and my people shall never be ashamed" (Joel 2:26-27). David was correct when he said: "For the LORD God is a sun and shield: the LORD will give grace and glory: *no good thing will he withhold from them that walk uprightly*" (Ps. 84:11). It has often been claimed that the famous vine at Hampton Court, London, was useless until its roots reached the river Thames. Then, suddenly, it became one of the most fruitful in the world. A similar fact may be claimed concerning superficial Christians. Jesus taught that unless the branches abide in the vine, fruitbearing would be impossible. Unless the trees, or vines, be filled with sap, their natural growth would be hindered. Similarly, it may be said that unless Christians draw continually from the wells of God's salvation (Isa. 12:2-3), productive service will be impossible.

This statement was first used as the theme of an angel's message. Since that time, it has been one of the most triumphant texts of the Christian church, and has been quoted by almost every pastor, teacher and evangelist.

Dr. Schmucker, when walking in the country, met an old man who was singing. He asked: "Father Miller, why should an old gentleman like you be so cheerful?" His friend replied: "Not all are, but I belong to the Lord." The questioner continued: "Are there many others like you?" "O no," came the response, "Listen to one who knows, for you will never find any man of three-score years and ten who will deny it. *The devil has no happy old men.*"

That simple, but truthful, statement was irrefutable. People in the twilight years of life may reminisce and be either proud or regretful, but looking into the unknown can be a frightening experience. An atheist who has no hope of eternal life can hardly be thrilled by the prospect of his imminent decease. He believes he will never again see a blue sky or a rainbow. The joys of watching flowers bloom and hearing the laughter of children remain unknown. His only assurance beyond death is that he will be buried, and his body will decay.

Stars of promise never brighten his skies, and no vestige of hope beckons his soul into eternity. He has lived a life without God, and remains a sinking human vessel without hope of rescue. To the contrary, it may be claimed that God has no miserable old people. Their terminal days on earth are bright with the assurance they are about to become young again!

Barzillai . . . *How Contented* (2 Sam. 19:34-35)

David was astounded; his aged friend was being obstinate. Why should he refuse the greatest offer ever made by a king? They had been together through the tempestuous days of Absalom's rebellion, and had survived his insurrection. Many of David's friends became deserters during the national crisis, but the faithfulness of Barzillai would never be forgotten. He had sustained the king and his followers, and had been loyal when others were traitors. David never expected to be able to repay this debt of love, but Jehovah had been gracious. The usurper prince was dead; the future shone with the prospect of total victory.

David smiled when he looked at his elderly benefactor. "And the king said unto Barzillai, Come thou over with me, and I will feed thee with me in Jerusalem." The king's eyes were bright as he thought of the continuing fellowship he planned to share with his loyal friend. Patiently, he awaited the old man's reply. There was silence on the roadway; even the soldiers were pleased. They liked the idea of favoring the man who had helped them during the rebellion.

> "And Barzillai said unto the king, How long have I to live, that I should go up with the king unto Jerusalem? I am this day four-score years old: and can I discern between good and evil? can thy servant taste what I eat, or what I drink? can I hear any more the voice of singing men and singing women? wherefore then should thy servant be yet a burden unto my lord the king? . . . Let thy servant turn back again, that I might die in mine own city, and be buried by the grave of my father, and of my mother" (2 Sam. 19:35, 37).

Arguments were useless; persuasion was a waste of time; the old man had made up his mind; his decision was final. He intended to return to the peacefulness of his home, where he would await an invitation to reside in another city which was eternal in the heavens (Heb. 11:10). Almost any other man in the kingdom would have welcomed a chance to accept David's offer, but Barzillai was not just another man! The pleasure to be found in the palace no longer attracted him; the music of trained singers was uninteresting; the plaudits of appreciative people fell on deaf ears. Nevertheless, he could hear the voice of God, especially in his home in the country. As Paul would have said, he had "set his affections on things above, not on things on the earth." Barzillai was both wise and wonderful. When, a little later, God came to escort him to the heavenly mansion, he was able to say: "Lord, I have been waiting for you," and they went home together!

Job . . . *How Convinced* (Job 19:25-27)

Job, as the entire world knows, had every reason to grumble. A deluge of trouble had devastated his family, and it was easy to believe God had gone on a vacation! It was perfectly natural for the man to long for death for that at least apparently would end his agony. He asked: "Why died I not from the womb? . . . For now should I have lain still and been quiet, I should have slept; then had I been at rest . . . There the wicked cease from troubling; and there the weary be at rest" (Job 3:11-17).

When Job, an elderly farmer, spoke those words, his understanding of truth was limited. He believed death to be an escape from pain and sorrow—to be eternally asleep was better than enduring daily anguish! His misery was unprecedented and inexplicable. God's testimony concerning Job was extremely interesting. "And the LORD said unto Satan, Hast thou considered my servant Job, that there is none like him in the earth, a perfect and an upright man, one that feareth God and escheweth evil?" (1:8). That statement suggested a man can be morally good even if his theological ideas remain undeveloped. At that period in his life, the patriarch had no incentive toward righteousness except an inherent love for virtue. The greatest lessons in life remained to be explained. Job was miserable—but things were about to happen.

God's greatest revelations resemble stars—they shine in the dark! As Job's daily problems accentuated and deepened, he began to think about eternity. If Jehovah were immortal, could He be satisfied if His children remained dead? He had no Bible to read; no preachers to hear; no meetings to attend. His conscience was a classroom, the Spirit of God his Teacher. Even before he realized what was taking place, Job began asking questions about immortality. He said: "If a man die, shall he live again? All the days of my appointed time will I wait, till my change come" (14:14). Was this the first time heaven's light shone into Job's darkened intellect? To what change was he referring? Was he expressing a hope that after his tribulation circumstances would improve, or was he thinking about survival? Evidently he believed his days had been appointed, therefore, God was still on His throne. The darkness was not as intense as hitherto! A man could never ask such a question and not endeavor to find its answer. It may never be known how Job discovered the truth of immortality, but his subsequent testimony indicated his doubts had gone; his questions had been answered. His night of anguish led to the dawn of a most wonderful day.

Job said: "And . . . though worms destroy this body, yet in my flesh shall I see God: Whom I shall see for myself, and mine eyes shall behold, and not another; though my reins be consumed within me" (Job 19:26-27). The Amplified Version translates the text: "And my eyes shall behold him, and not as a stranger. *My heart pines away and is consumed within me.*" His discovery made his future attractive: even his physical suffering was less consequential. Job was consumed with a desire to possess his new body, and see the Redeemer who would stand upon the earth. He had changed dramatically, and had become one of God's happy old men. Job's night of suffering terminated when the Sun of Righteousness arose with healing in His wings (Mal. 4:2).

Paul . . . *How Confident* (2 Tim. 4:7-8)

"Henceforth there is laid up for me a crown of righteousness, which the Lord, the righteous judge, shall give me at that day: and not to me only, but unto all them also that love his appearing."

We do not know the apostle's age when he wrote this letter to Timothy. He was nearing the end of his life, and at the time was a prisoner in Rome. Paul had succeeded in cramming four lifetimes into one. He had traversed the world of his day, and was known in almost every city, town and village; and he had become prematurely old. The record of experiences chills the human spirit, for he wrote: ". . . in labors more abundant, in stripes above measure, in prisons more frequent, in deaths oft. Of the Jews five times received I forty stripes save one. Thrice was I beaten with rods, once was I stoned, thrice I suffered shipwreck, a night and a day have I been in the deep; In journeyings often, in perils of waters, in perils of robbers, in perils by mine own countrymen, in perils by the heathen, in perils in the city, in perils in the wilderness, in perils in the sea, in perils among false brethren; In weariness and painfulness, in watchings often, in hunger and thirst, in fastings often, in cold and nakedness. . ." (2 Cor. 11:23-27).

It was remarkable that the intrepid traveler never complained, and he only itemized the list of sufferings to silence critics. After years of hazardous service, Paul had grown old. Through cold and terrible winters, he traveled to reach unevangelized areas, and millions of people heard the gospel from his lips. His earthly ministry had apparently terminated in a Roman prison, but he was not discouraged, and even in a rented apartment, he continued to tell visitors about the matchless grace of God (Acts 28:30-31).

The great missionary realized his earthly career would soon terminate; he would become a martyr. He had no regrets; his spirit was about to be released from earthly bondage, and within moments, would be on the way to a heavenly home. He wrote: "The time of my departure is at hand." Paul did not say: "The time of my death is near"; neither did he say: "Henceforth there awaits me a casket, or a criminal's grave." The word translated *departure* was an interesting Greek word made up of two components. *Analuseos* was formed from a prefix and a verb, which meant *to loose*. The prefix added another thought— *to go on a journey*. It was difficult for the translators to supply a word which expressed *to be liberated*, and *to go on a journey*.

My father, in the early days of his marriage, possessed eighty racing pigeons, and was well known for his trophies. As a small child I questioned his method of selecting a bird for a special race. When I expressed my objections, I was told I did not understand; when I persisted in interfering with my father's methods, I was physically reminded he was the boss!

I have often imagined the pigeon enclosed in a basket hundreds of miles from home, and awaiting the moment when the container would be opened. If it were possible to read that bird's thoughts, they would have been twofold: (1) *I want to get out of this basket; I want to be released*; (2) *I want to start my journey. My babies are waiting, and the more quickly I start my flight, the sooner I shall see them again.*

The word *analuseo* perfectly expressed Paul's desire. He wanted to be released from his body to begin his journey to heaven; a loved one awaited his arrival. When the apostle thought of his arrival in heaven his face reflected the joy of his soul. He was anything but miserable.

An elderly man was dying in Edinburgh, Scotland. His drinking and gambling friends stood around watching their ailing comrade. One of them leaned over the bed and said: "Harry, hold on!" The sick man whispered, "What did you say?" and the message was repeated: "Hold on!" After a moment the reply came; "I have nothing to hold on to!" Father Miller was correct when he said: "The Devil has no happy old men."

During World War II, thousands of children were evacuated from London to find new homes in the country. To them it was the greatest adventure of their lives; they left little of value in the dirty and dangerous suburbs of the British metropolis. One of those boys came to live with my parents in Crosskeys, Monmouthshire. His arrival almost caused a panic. He was proud of his new shoes, but, unfortunately, he had never seen a bath and considered them to be excellent skate boards with which to slide from the shallow end toward the sink! Day after day my mother's blood pressure reached record levels. Many stories could be told of the reactions of those refugee children to the way of life they discovered away from the gloom and depression of the suburbs of London. One day, a small boy looked up and exclaimed, "Oooooooh! What a big sky they've got 'ere." He had been overshadowed by the tall dirty buildings of his old home, and had never seen the vast expanse of the heavens. In the country, where there were no towering buildings, the little fellow could see the far-reaching sky, and the view filled him with awe.

There are innumerable people who have never appreciated the greatness of God's grace. They live in the shadows where the outlook is bleak and forbidding. When they first discover the immensity of the Lord's provision their souls are filled with astonishment.

His great love . . . *Informing* . . . (Eph. 2:4)

"But God, who is rich in mercy, for *his great love* wherewith he loved us, Even when we were dead in sins, hath quickened us together with Christ." The importance of this statement may be seen in the answers to three simple questions. (1) Why? — *"God was rich in mercy."* Mankind had disappointed the Creator and deserved judgment. Yet the Lord continued to love sinners, and nothing could prevent His endeavor to regain what had been lost. (2) When? — *"Even when we were dead in sins."* Since sinners were *"dead"* in sins, they could do nothing to save themselves. Hence the statement "By grace are ye saved"

(Eph. 2:5). Paul said: "For when we were yet without strength, in due time Christ died for the ungodly. For scarcely for a righteous man will one die; yet peradventure for a good man some would even dare to die. But God commendeth his love toward us, in that, while we were yet sinners, Christ died for us" (Rom. 5:6-8). (3) What? — *"He hath quickened us together with Christ . . . and hath raised us up together, and made us sit together in heavenly places, in Christ Jesus. That in the ages to come he might shew the exceeding riches of his grace in his kindness toward us through Christ Jesus"* (Eph. 2:5-7). Probably this statement was one of the most comprehensive ever made by the apostle. It included *the past* — "when we were dead in sins, he quickened us"; *the present* — "And hath raised us up together with Christ and made us sit together in heavenly places in Christ Jesus . . ."; *the future* — "That in the ages to come he might shew the exceeding riches of his grace in his kindness toward us through Christ Jesus." The love of God is all-embracing.

His Great Salvation . . . *Insisting* . . . (Heb. 2:3-4)

The writer to the Hebrews asked the only unanswerable question in the Bible. "How shall we escape, if we neglect so great salvation; which at the first began to be spoken by the Lord, and was confirmed unto us by them that heard him; God also bearing them witness, both with signs and wonders, and with diverse miracles, and gifts of the Holy Spirit according to his own will?" There never can be any escape for those who reject God's greatest gift. It is significant that the Son *expressed* the Gospel—". . . which at the first began to be spoken by the Lord." The Father *endorsed* it — "God also bearing them witness." The Holy Spirit *emphasized* it—". . . with gifts of the Holy Ghost according to his own will."

Each member of the divine Family helped to propagate the greatest story ever told. Jewish law insisted favor with the Almighty depended on human merit. The only righteousness known was obtained through conformity to Hebrew law; and since it was impossible to obey the innumerable details of legal requirements, men had no hope of eternal salvation. The Savior announced forgiveness was given freely; that justification was obtained through faith and not works. God sacrificed His Son to provide salvation, and to reject this superlative offer would be suicidal. There would never be another way to obtain eternal security. It was this indisputable truth which made Paul say: "But though we, or an angel from heaven, preach any other gospel unto you than that which we have preached unto you, let him be accursed" (Gal. 1:8).

His Great Power . . . *Imparted* . . . (Acts 4:33)

"And with great power gave the apostles witness of the resurrection of the Lord Jesus. . . ." Throughout the history of the church, sceptics challenged the fact of the resurrection, and all kinds of inconclusive arguments were advanced to prove Jesus of Nazareth remained dead. Unfortunately, most of the antagonists never considered that probably the greatest proof of Christ's resurrection was the amazing change which transformed weaklings into giants! It was written that all the disciples forsook the Lord and fled (Mark 14:50). Yet, those same disciples became new men! Simon Peter, who was scared by a maid, and who, consequently, feared for his life, became a dynamic preacher who, on the day of Pentecost, confronted thousands of enraged listeners caring not whether he lived or died. Timid people became bold, and forgetting their fears, went into the arena to sing as they died. When Nero tried to exterminate Christianity, he burned saints in the palace gardens, but the fire within the hearts of the martyrs surpassed anything kindled by the emperor. If the resurrection of Christ did not happen, it would be interesting to discover what changed the early believers.

The spiritual dynamic of the early church might be summarized under three headings.

(1) *They had power to speak* both to God and men. None of the original disciples studied in a theological college, and there is no evidence they had been convincing public speakers. Peter and John were ordinary fishermen, and were only experienced in the art of discussing the weather and prospects of excellent fishing. Yet, these men suddenly ranked among the world's greatest orators. Fearlessly, they addressed the learned leaders

of the Sanhedrin, and their knowledge of the Scriptures was amazing.

(2) *They had power to save.* When asked by a beggar at the temple to supply a gift of money, ". . . Peter, fastening his eyes upon him with John, said, Look on us. And he gave heed unto them, expecting to receive something of them. Then Peter said, Silver and gold have I none: but such as I have give I thee: In the name of Jesus Christ of Nazareth rise up and walk. And he took him by the right hand, and lifted him up. And immediately his feet and ankle bones received strength. And he leaping up stood, and walked, and entered with them into the temple, walking, and leaping, and praising God" (Acts 3:4-8). Probably those men had performed miracles earlier when in the Name of their Master they preached in the villages of Palestine. Yet, at that time, they were very conscious of the presence and power of their Lord. Later, they stood alone — or did they? Their Master was still alive — living within their souls.

(3) *They had power to sacrifice.* People can be extremely selfish. Yet the early Christians were ". . . of one heart, and of one soul: neither said any of them that ought of the things which he possessed was his own; but they had all things common. . . . Neither was there any among them that lacked: for as many as were possessors of lands or houses sold them, and brought the prices of the things that were sold. And laid them down at the apostles' feet: and distribution was made unto every man according as he had need" (Acts 4:32, 34-35).

His Great Grace . . . *Influencing* (Acts 4:33)

". . . *and great grace was upon them all.*" It would be impossible to overestimate the economic problems which confronted the early believers. Their conversion to Christianity meant loss of jobs and income. As time progressed, the inevitability of choice became a challenge to their unity. When Ananias and Sapphira died because of their deception, relatives or friends could have vehemently disagreed with the sentence imposed by Peter. This may have been exceedingly damaging to the harmony of the first church. Even the leaders were not immune from temptation, and this became evident when Paul and Barnabas disagreed about John Mark's reinstatement into the missionary party (Acts 15:37-41). The membership of the early church was diverse, for men and women of many nations had been initiated into a fellowship previously unknown. People were different in every age, and their thoughts and actions were very provocative. Unless great grace had filled the souls of the Christians, the unity of the church would have been impossible.

The people shared their resources and gave without hesitation; they never asked if certain recipients deserved assistance, nor inquired how to benefit personally by their sacrifice. When problems arose, they did not convene a special meeting in which to criticize the decisions of superiors. They did not divide the church in Jerusalem. When arguments had to be settled, people met humbly at the foot of the cross "and great grace was upon them all."

The Great High Priest . . . *Interceding* (Heb. 4:14)

"Seeing then that we have a great high priest, that is passed into the heavens, Jesus the Son of God, let us hold fast our profession." Most of the converts won for Christ on the day of Pentecost were acquainted with priestly representation. Even though many lived in foreign countries, they knew the priest acted on their behalf each time he ministered within the temple. When they accepted the new doctrines, they gained an entirely new conception of the intercessory work of the Lord. His ministry exceeded anything they had known.

(1) *Christ was greater than the Aaronic priests in that His ministry was not terminated by death.* "By so much was Jesus made a surety of a better testament. And they truly were many priests, because they were not suffered to continue by reason of death: But this man, because he continueth ever, hath an unchangeable priesthood" (Heb. 7:22-24).

(2) *Christ was greater in that He was personally acquainted with those He represented.* "For we have not an high priest which cannot be touched with the feeling of our infirmities; but was in all points tempted like as we are, yet without sin" (Heb. 4:15).

(3) *Christ was greater because He was always accessible to His people.* This was unknown during the Aaronic priesthood.

51

"Let us come boldly unto the throne of grace, that we may obtain mercy, and find grace to help in time of need" (Heb. 4:16).

(4) *Christ was greater in that He went into heaven to appear directly before the throne of God.* "For Christ is not entered into the holy places made with hands, which are the figures of the true; but into heaven itself, now to appear in the presence of God for us" (Heb. 9:24).

(5) *Christ was greater in that He did not offer the blood of animals — He offered His own blood.* "Neither by the blood of goats and calves, but by his own blood he entered in once into the holy place, having obtained eternal redemption for us" (Heb. 9:12).

(6) *Christ was greater in that He was more than human — He was born of God.* ". . . his Son . . . Who being the brightness of his glory, and the express image of his person, and upholding all things by the word of his power, when he had by himself purged our sins, sat down on the right hand of the Majesty on high" (Heb. 1:2-3).

(7) *Christ was greater than any other priest, for He did not offer many sacrifices—He offered Himself once, and that was sufficient.* "Nor yet that he should offer himself often, as the high priest entereth into the holy place every year with blood of others: For then must he often have suffered since the foundation of the world: but now once in the end of the world hath he appeared to put away sin by the sacrifice of himself" (Heb. 9:12, 25-28). It is extremely doubtful whether any other priest was ever called "great."

His Great Shepherd . . . *Inviting* (Heb. 13:20-21)

"Now the God of peace, that brought again from the dead our Lord Jesus, that great shepherd of the sheep, through the blood of the everlasting covenant; Make you perfect in every good work to do his will, working in you that which is well pleasing in his sight. . . ." The Savior was called *the Good Shepherd Who redeems* (John 10:11); *the Great Shepherd Who responds* (Heb. 13:20); *the Chief Shepherd Who rewards* (1 Peter 5:4). A true shepherd supplies three things for his sheep.

Devotion. It would be more desirable to sleep in a warm bed than to lie beneath a hedge, or behind a wall. The shepherd knew His flock, and was able to call the sheep. His voice was recognized, and his commands obeyed. His staying with the sheep at all times indicated they were considered a vital part of his life; he loved them.

Direction. It was the shepherd's duty to find suitable pasture. A Bedouin leads his sheep, goats or camels over great areas of his desertlike surroundings; without his guidance the animals would starve. When one pasture becomes inadequate, he leads to another, and as long as the animals follow his guidance, their future is assured.

Defense. When David was a shepherd on the hills of Bethlehem, he fought against a lion and a bear. If the sheep were in the sheepfold, he lay in the doorway; if they roamed the hills, he protected them against all enemies. When they were sick, he cradled their heads in his arms and remained with them as long as it was necessary. It was significant Jesus said: "My sheep hear my voice, and I know them, and they follow me" (John 10:27). The apostle Peter urged the elders the church to "Feed the flock of God which is among you . . ." (1 Peter 5:2). Christ was able to supply what was expected of a good and great leader. This fact gave increasing value to His invitation: "Come unto me all ye that labour and are heavy laden, and I will give you rest" (Matt. 11:28).

His Great Promises . . . *Inspiring* (2 Peter 1:4)

"Whereby are given unto us exceeding great and precious promises: that by these ye might be partakers of the divine nature, having escaped the corruption that is in the world through lust." Webster's Dictionary defines a promise as "*An oral or written agreement to do or not to do something—a vow. To give a basis for hopes or expectation.*" Obviously, many promises are either broken or forgotten. Sincere people regard a vow as a pledge never to be violated; a guarantee of fulfillment. The Savior commanded His disciples to ". . . wait for the promise of the Father . . ." (Acts 14). Those words were fulfilled at Pentecost, but the guarantee that it would happen was based on the immutability of God. He never broke any of His promises. The veracity of His word and the reliability of His covenants remained unbroken since the beginning of time.

Peter evidently had difficulty in expressing himself. He might have referred to the promises of God as "precious" but the term seemed inadequate. Then he wrote "great and precious promises," but even that did not satisfy him. The apostle considered for a moment and finally wrote: "*exceeding* great and precious promises. . . ." Had he been asked "How great? how exceeding?" he might have lifted his hands in despair. It is impossible to measure infinity; and it is useless trying to express the inexpressible.

The Bible supplies promises to help the young, the very old, and others who are between the two extremes. David was correct when he wrote: "Thy word is a lamp unto my feet, and a light unto my path" (Ps. 119:105).

His Great City . . . *Incredible* (Rev. 21:10)

"And he carried me away in the spirit to a great and high mountain, and shewed me that great city, the holy Jerusalem, descending out of heaven from God." The Holy City will be the greatest architectural achievement of all ages. Its characteristics may be summarized under five headings:

(1) *Its Great Size.* The Savior said: "In my Father's house are many mansions [dwelling places]; if it were not so, I would have told you. I go to prepare a place for you" (John 14:2). The city of which He spoke was mentioned by the apostle John, who wrote: "And the city lieth foresquare, and the length is as large as the breadth: and he measured the city with the reed, twelve thousand furlongs. The length and the breadth and the height thereof are equal" (Rev. 21:16). There has never been a city to be compared with that which will be the center of attraction throughout eternity. If it descended today, it would cover two-thirds of the United States of America (see the author's book *What in the World Will Happen Next?*, pgs. 175-176).

(2) *Its Great Significance.* "And the nations of them which are saved shall walk in the light of it; and the kings of the earth do bring their glory and honor into it" (Rev. 21:24). This is a

remarkable statement for it reveals events to happen throughout eternity. Peter said: "Nevertheless we, according to his promise, look for new heavens and *a new earth*, wherein dwelleth righteousness" (2 Peter 3:13). Evidently upon that new earth will be a race of sinless beings; there will be kings and governments, but the population of the entire earth will pay homage to the King of Kings.

(3) *Its Great Sovereign.* The Son of God Who will reign upon earth for a thousand years, will continue His reign forever. It was written: ". . . the saints would see His face" (Rev. 22:4). The citizens of the eternal city will also see the population of the New Earth coming to worship their Lord. When Christ first came to earth, "He came unto his own, and his own received him not" (John 1:11). Throughout eternity everybody will accept, love and serve Him.

(4) *Its Great Serenity.* "And the gates of the city shall not be shut at all by day: for there shall be no night there. And they shall bring the glory and honour of the nations into it. And there shall in no wise enter into it anything that defileth, neither whatsoever worketh abomination, or maketh a lie: but they which are written in the Lamb's book of life" (Rev. 21:25-27). Within the city of the King there will never be a hospital; a cemetery; a retirement home for the aged; a doctor's office; a prison.

(5) *Its Great Security.* ". . . the kingdoms of this world are become the kingdoms of our Lord, and of his Christ; and he shall reign for ever and ever" (Rev. 11:15). Finite minds cannot comprehend the magnitude of God's provision for His people. It is difficult to understand how the Holy City will be fifteen hundred miles high, and appreciate all that will take place within it. Its wonder will never diminish, and age cannot threaten its continuance. God's far-reaching kindness is beyond comprehension.

Spiritual hunger begets intense yearning for fellowship with God. It may be true to say few people attain to that exalted position. David exclaimed: "As the hart panteth after the water-brooks, so panteth my soul after thee, O God" (Ps. 42:1). During droughts in South Africa, I often watched the springboks (deer) defying lions in order to drink at the river. Their unquenchable thirst could not be denied. Water had to be obtained or survival was impossible. When men and women seek after God with the same intensity, their spiritual status becomes immeasurable.

Six kinds of hunger may be found in human beings. Hunger (1) For food and raiment, which produces harvests, tools and industrial activities. (2) For knowledge, which produces schools, books, papers and literature. (3) For fame, which produces office, rank, political parties and spheres of influence. (4) For beauty, which creates the fine arts, and encourages inherent capabilities. (5) For affection, which creates homes, fireside songs and acts of service which could never develop without love. (6) There can and should be hunger for God; the intimate relationship which joins heaven and earth, and unites the Creator and the created in a family where love is predominant. This is the greatest of all, for when people are in tune with the Almighty, all yearning is satisfied by the Lord of Heaven. The man who hungers after righteousness rarely desires lesser things.

A Gracious Promise (Matt. 5:6)

"Blessed are they which do hunger and thirst after righteousness; for they shall be filled." This was the fourth of the nine beatitudes which formed the basis of the new morality embraced by the Christian church. Probably, the greatest example of hungering after God was provided by the Savior. Conscious of His continuing need, Jesus often rose early in the morning to commune with His Father. Throughout most of His days the Lord was fully occupied attending to the needs of sick people, but the outflow of Divine energy had to be matched by an inflow of spiritual power, and the only way this could be maintained was through continuing fellowship with God.

Christ hungered for something earth could not supply. He said to His disciples: "Blessed are they which do hunger and thirst after righteousness: for they shall be filled." That yearning, in itself, was the guarantee God would supply what was necessary. The rich young ruler hungered for financial security; Pharisees sought the praises of men; athletes long for greater success in their chosen careers; financiers seek greater profit in their investments; politicians work for important positions in government, but true Christians desire to be Christlike. They are the only people confident of reaching their objectives in life.

A Great Preventative (John 6:35)

"And Jesus said unto them, I am the bread of life: he that cometh to me shall never hunger; and he that believeth on me shall never thirst." When the children of Israel wandered in the wilderness, they were sustained by manna provided by God. Nevertheless, the people were commanded to collect daily supplies. They gathered twice as much on the eve of the Sabbath, and the food never perished.

Deprived of daily sustenance, the nation would have died. It was significant when Jesus claimed to be the equivalent of the food sent from heaven. He said: ". . . Moses gave you that bread from heaven; but my Father giveth you the true bread from heaven. For the bread of God is he that cometh down from heaven, and giveth life unto the world" (John 6:32-33). Jesus promised that if and when people came to Him, He would satisfy their longings and solve their problems. He reiterated the same truth when He said: "Come unto me, all ye that labor and are heavy laden, and I will give you rest" (Matt. 11:28).

He claimed He had the ability to supply His followers' needs, and history proved He was correct. Christians who abide in His presence remain satisfied. It is only when men forsake the Savior that they experience impoverishment, and lust after what the scripture calls *"the fleshpots of Egypt."* No other person was able to do what Jesus did.

Many years ago, *The Christian Evangelist* published a story about a little street-girl who became ill at Christmastime. She

57

was taken to the hospital where she heard, for the first time, the story of the birth of Jesus. One day, when the nurse came on her round of duty, "Little Broomstick"—that was the child's street name—held her hand and whispered: "Nurse, I am having real good times here, ever such good times. S'pose I'll have to go 'way from here as soon as I get well; but I'll take the good times along—some of it, anyhow! Did you know about Jesus being born?"

"Yes" replied the nurse, "I know, but you must not talk anymore."

The child replied: "You did! I thought you looked as if you didn't, and I was going to tell you."

"Why, how did I look?" inquired the nurse. The little girl said: "Oh, just like most folk—kind o' glum. I shouldn't think you'd ever look glum if you'd knowed about Jesus being born."

A Glorious Provision (Rev. 7:16)

"After this, I beheld, and, lo, a great multitude, which no man could number, of all nations, and kindreds, and people, and tongues, stood before the throne, and before the Lamb . . . and he said to me, These are they which came out of great tribulation, and have washed their robes, and made them white in the blood of the Lamb . . . they shall hunger no more, neither thirst any more . . . for the Lamb which is in the midst of the throne shall feed them, and shall lead them unto living fountains of water: and God shall wipe away all tears from their eyes" (Rev. 7:9-17).

The scene mentioned by John described believers already in heaven. The apostle emphasized they would neither hunger nor thirst because the Lamb of God had assumed responsibility for supplying their eternal need. The river of the water of life could never run dry, for it came from the heart of God, and was eternal. It is very difficult at this stage of the Christian journey to assess what might, or might not, be needed. The King of Kings will provide every requirement in the hereafter as efficiently as He did when the church was upon earth. The revised form of the old Welsh hymn expresses this important fact:

> Bread of Heaven; Bread of Heaven
> Feed me now and *evermore*.

There is no sadder sight than that of a professing Christian without a desire for the deeper things of God, whose only interests are unspiritual.

Robert Robinson, the author of the beloved hymn, *Come Thou Fount of Every Blessing*, unfortunately, lost his hunger and thirst after God, and for most of his declining years, strayed from the Lord. He became deeply disturbed, and, hoping to find relief in travel, decided to visit foreign lands.

During one of his journeys he met a young woman who was interested in poetry. She asked what he thought of a hymn she had just been reading. He was astonished to discover she had become interested in his own composition. Robinson tried to evade her question, but she persisted in requesting his answer.

Suddenly, he began to weep. As the tears streamed down his face, the author confessed that he had written those lines many years earlier. He said: "I would give anything to experience now the joy I knew then." Although greatly surprised, the young woman assured him, *the streams of mercy* mentioned in his song *still flowed*. He was deeply moved, and *turning his wandering heart to the Lord*, was restored to fellowship with Christ. It was only then he realized the blessedness of his own words.

> O to grace how great a debtor
> Daily I'm constrained to be
> Let Thy goodness, like a fetter
> Bind my wandering heart to Thee.
> Prone to wander, Lord, I feel it;
> Prone to leave the God I love;
> Here's my heart, O take and seal it,
> Seal it for Thy courts above.

Throughout the Middle East flies are a nuisance. They invade houses, annoy travelers and contaminate produce. I have walked through markets in Egypt and watched thousands of the pests crawling over the displays in the butchers' shops. I shuddered when native customers, accustomed to the sight, drove off the winged menace and eagerly bought the meat.

Thankfully, the Israeli Ministry of Health made protective laws which changed this condition in their country, but centuries ago, during the reign of Solomon, myriads of flies were a national problem. The king's statement concerning *flies in the ointment* became famous, and now belongs to every man's vocabulary.

When Solomon heard of the event in the shop of the royal perfumer, he probably smiled, but even he could not have guessed his musings on the matter were to become internationally famous in all ages. The needs of the royal court made great demands upon the apothecaries, for Solomon delighted in an abundance of female companions!

The following outline is a brief summary of the study found in the author's book *Bible Treasures*, pgs. 53 and 54 (published by Kregel Publications, Grand Rapids, MI).

The Ointment Unspoiled

The manufacturer was pleased with himself. He had perfected fragrance. The perfume exceeded anything previously known. The many queens and associates of the king would pay handsomely for the newest sensation. Was the man unexpectedly called away? Did some other problem precipitate itself into the mind of the satisfied apothecary? Surely something of the sort happened, for no fly could get into the ointment unless *the lid had been left off the box.*

The Ointment Unguarded

In a land where flies were, and still are, bred by the millions; where the winged nuisances succeed in annoying everybody, it would not be long before those wretched things were attracted to the box of loveliness. Why didn't that stupid man put the lid on the box? He should have known that presents for royalty should be protected.

The Ointment Unexamined

We could forgive the perfumer if an unexpected call interfered with his work; if some momentary forgetfulness intervened. Alas, it is impossible to forgive the inexcusable. A fly going into the ointment is not sufficient to make it stink! No ointment can deteriorate instantly. If the ointment be revolting, *then the flies were permitted to stay in it*. The satisfied apothecary did not return to examine the product until the invaders had ruined the product . . . probably this kind of thing had happened before. It has certainly happened since. Dead flies can ruin any ointment.

The Ointment Unattractive

What a shame! That illustrious box might have graced the boudoir of the Queen of Sheba. Mr. Perfumer, why did you not put the lid on that box? Yes, we know what you are thinking — why don't we do likewise when our best gifts are ready for the King of kings? Ananias and Sapphira had a rare gift, but they went away to sell a house when they might have been killing flies! There were others who suffered loss because pests ruined their ointment.

John Mark . . . *The Fly That Disturbed His Serenity* (Acts 13:13)

He was a privileged young man, envied by all the young people in the church in Jerusalem. His uncle Barnabas was a prominent leader among the Christians, and had opened the door of adventure and fame for his excited nephew. Each time John Mark attended a service, people smiled at him; his future was bright with prospect and hope. Possibly he would become great like his famous uncle, but, in any case, he would see the world in all its fascinating wonder. Perhaps on the night before departure, a special farewell party was arranged in his honor,

61

and the following day, accompanied by Paul and Barnabas, he began his travels for Christ. Alas, the first two journeys were overseas. First he went to Cyprus, and after a brief stay on the island, to Perga in Pamphylia, where unfortunately, the lad encountered a swarm of flies! "Now when Paul and his company loosed from Paphos, they came to Perga in Pamphylia: *and John departing from them returned to Jerusalem*" (Acts 13:13).

How can that premature departure be explained? There are seven possible answers. (1) Had he been seasick on his voyages? Did that experience destroy his love for travel? (2) Had he become homesick? Was he missing his mother who had — perhaps — spoiled him? (3) Was he upset because Paul had become the leader of their party? Did he resent the newly acquired authority of Paul? (4) Was he fearful of the future? Their itinerary would go through hostile territory where danger abounded. (5) Did he resent the fact that their ministry was among Gentiles? He was a Jew. (6) Was he disappointed with his work? He dreamed of becoming a great preacher, and not an excellent washer of dirty dishes. (7) Did he realize he was not meant to be an itinerant preacher; that he had embarked upon a task to which God had not called him? (See the author's commentary on *The Amazing Acts*, pgs. 221-222).

It may be difficult to decide which of these suggestions may be correct, but one conclusion is unavoidable, John Mark had been pestered by a swarm of flies; they had caused discomfort, spoiled his vision, and destroyed his serenity. As Solomon would have said — for a while at least, his ointment was ruined — it began to exude an offensive odor.

Demas . . . *The Fly That Disrupted His Service* (2 Tim. 4:10)

Demas was frustrated and irritable; something was seriously wrong. Paul, within his prison cell, had retired for the night. The Mamertine prison in Rome reveals the terrible conditions in which the apostle lived out his last days. There was no sanitation; the air was unfit to be breathed; his food was let down through an opening in the stony ceiling. The young assistant had attended to the wishes of his master, but now, wrapped in the silence of the night, he was alone with his thoughts. He sighed; the outlook was intensely bleak. Apparently, there would never be any more thrilling evangelistic meetings; the crowds had disappeared forever. It would only be a matter of time before Paul's execution. The thoughtful young man frowned and silently asked, "What will happen to me after he has gone?"

Within a few yards of the prison were crowded streets, attractive companions, and entertainment which continued throughout the night. Why should he waste his time caring for an old man? There were other Christians in Rome; why did they not share the burden which he carried? Even Paul had admitted: "Only Luke is with me" (2 Tim. 4:11). Perhaps Demas sat down and placed his head into upturned hands. Outside the streets were filled with gaiety, but his soul was flooded with the blackness of despair. Poor Demas, he had forgotten to replace the lid on his box of very precious ointment!

Perhaps he had secretly visited the glamorous places in Rome, and unfortunately had been attracted by what he had seen. It has often been claimed that mosquitos carry the disease of sleeping sickness. It would seem the flies which damaged the soul of that youthful attendant brought a similar illness to his soul. His eyes became less alert; his shoulders sagged; his spiritual perception disappeared. Yes, he knew what he would do. Let others sacrifice their time to help the imprisoned preacher. Demas arose and walked into oblivion.

Judas ... *The Fly That Destroyed His Soul* (John 13:30)

It is always sad when a soldier falls on the field of battle, but his death might not change the ultimate result of the war. When a general is slain, it is sometimes difficult to replace the fallen leader. The same thing applies to the Christian church. It is to be regretted when any believer in Christ becomes a victim of evil, but when a minister, or a prominent worker for the Lord collapses, the effect upon the extension of Christ's kingdom is tragic. The treachery of Judas Iscariot left a stain upon the conscience of the church which time could not erase. Poor Judas was not only attacked by a deadly insect; he was killed by a dragon-fly!

There is reason to believe Judas worked as hard as any other disciple when, with a companion, he went forth to preach in the villages of Palestine. He firmly believed his Master would be the Messiah, and few would question his sincerity when he announced the kingdom of heaven was at hand. Perhaps it is foolish to ask: "What might Judas have become had he retained his earliest convictions?" It is true he robbed the treasury; that he took much needed money from the gifts received from well wishers. He could have been forgiven for that initial dishonesty, but unfortunately, having stolen successfully, he developed the habit which destroyed his soul.

Judas anticipated the coronation of his Master, and began planning the role he would play in the establishment of Christ's domain. His eyes were bright when he thought of future glory; he was sure he would be indispensable in the ongoing work of God's kingdom. His anticipatory joys vanished when Jesus indicated He would never wage war against the Romans. Judas could not believe his ears, and slowly his eagerness changed to disillusionment. He had wasted his time grasping a bubble!

Within his warped mind he thought: *God helps those who help themselves.* And at that moment, Hell's dragon-fly attacked him. It is difficult to decide the quality of the ointment stored within his box, but whether it was extremely valuable or ordinary, Judas did not protect it — he left the lid off the box, and throughout succeeding ages, his name became obnoxious. It was truly a very dark night when the demented man committed suicide. He had walked into a dark tunnel at the end of which was no light! "He went out, and it was night."

Mary . . . *The Fly That Disliked Her Scrutiny*

Mary of Bethany was one of the most gracious ladies of her generation; she excelled in everything noble. Some commentators believe she belonged to a wealthy family, but that conclusion cannot be substantiated. It would appear that one of her greatest treasures was a box of very expensive ointment or perfume, but how she acquired this has never been ascertained. Possibly she saved her money and bought it. On the other hand, it could have been a present from Martha and Lazarus or a would-be husband. It may never be known how often within the privacy of her own room she examined her treasure and inhaled its fragrance.

The delightful woman was always careful to replace the lid on her box. Her treasure should never be destroyed by the winged monsters she could not exclude from her home. Her constant attention was rewarded when she took the box to the home of Simon, the leper, to pour its contents upon the feet of Jesus. She was determined the Lord should receive the best she had to offer.

Her sacrifice was a sweet-smelling savour which ascended to heaven. The Savior's eyes were pools of delight when He said: "Verily I say unto you, Wheresoever this gospel shall be preached in the whole world, there shall also this, that this woman hath done, be told for a memorial of her" (Matt. 26:13).

Fly-swatters are excellent, but it is wise to keep lids on all boxes—where they belong.

During the American Civil War, it became urgently necessary to send a message to the general in charge of operations on the firing line. An officer in the Union Army instructed his son to ride into the battle area, and when he returned, the father embraced the messenger and said: "I did not want to see you killed, but I needed someone I could trust."

Ezekiel's statement provided a thought-provoking word picture. Throughout the nation, cities, sheepfolds and vineyards were protected by walls. If these were broken, enemies could attack through the breaches and people lost their possessions. To break down a wall was an inexcusable crime. The prophet used that fact to impress upon his listeners a tremendous truth. The battle against the Babylonians had already been lost; the walls had been broken. Yet, the greatest peril was Israel's sin, and not the heathen invaders. Righteousness was about to pour through the breached walls to slay the guilty nation. God wanted to save His people, and had looked for a man who would prevent the threatened disaster. Unfortunately, such a deliverer could not be found, and the prophet's words became a window through which much could be seen.

The Strange Desire . . . *How Wise*

Moses was furious! Even Aaron was frightened when he said: "Let not the anger of my lord wax hot" (Exod. 32:22). The patriarch had been in the mountain with Jehovah, but his prolonged absence had become an excuse for Israel's idolatry. The people had requested the making of a golden calf that they might worship a god whom they could see. Women sacrificed their golden trinkets and necklaces; search was made throughout the camp for every ornament of value, and most of the people forgot their deliverance from Egypt.

When Moses descended from the holy mountain, he found it difficult to believe what he saw and heard. Serenity had been replaced by sinning and inspiration by idolatry. When his amazement subsided, indignation filled the patriarch's soul. "And it came to pass, as soon as he came nigh unto the camp, he saw the calf, and the dancing: and Moses' anger waxed hot, and he cast the tables out of his hands, and break them beneath the mount" (Exod. 32:19). That was one of the most desperate moments in Israel's history. Judgment appeared to be inevitable, but God found a man to stand in the gap (Exod. 32:32)!

The Stumbling Deliverer . . . *How Weak!*

It was inconceivable that the Israelites had survived twenty years of Philistine domination. Their enemies had been merciless tyrants who destroyed villages, confiscated crops and murdered innocent people. A different kind of Goliath had arisen, and the overwhelming superiority of the heathen had subdued and terrified the Hebrews—but—God found a man to stand in the gap!

Samson was unique, challenging and attractive, but arrogant and foolish. Temporarily he ceased being concerned with the plight of his people, and appeared to be mesmerized by a woman. "And it came to pass, when she pressed him daily with her words, and urged him, so that his soul was vexed unto death; That he told her all his heart, and said unto her, There hath not come a razor upon my head; for I have been a Nazarite unto God from my mother's womb: if I be shaven then my strength will go from me, and I shall become weak, *and be like any other man*" (Judges 16:16-17). Samson's phenomenal strength was not primarily in his uncut hair. His vows of consecration had never been broken. Other men might have had long hair and remained ordinary individuals. He was God's man, whose dedicated soul explained his dynamic strength. Alas, he failed, and as he predicted, became like any other man. God had found a man only to lose him to an enchantress.

The Surprising Delay . . . *How Woeful*

The disciples were jubilant; their Master's promise had been fulfilled. They had watched His ascent into heaven, and had experienced the thrill of Pentecost. Thousands of listeners had yielded to the claims of the Savior, and the future seemed bright with prospect and hope. The eyes of the preachers shone with happiness; the church had been established, but, unfortunately, its leaders remained complacent and forgetful. Christ had said: ". . . Go ye into all the world, and preach the gospel to every creature . . ." (Mark 16:15), but apparently the importance of that commission had been ignored.

They were content to remain in Jerusalem as administrators, and after fifteen years of complacency, enjoyed the comparative quietness of their surroundings. Christ won many disciples, but not one was equal to the challenge of world evangelism. It seemed His search for that type of man had been in vain. The Lord could have repeated His statement: "I sought for a man among them, that should . . . stand in the gap before me . . . but I found none." Then God searched again and found Saul of Tarsus.

The Stirred Disciple . . . *How Wonderful*

The city was in an uproar; a mob of angry people had rushed a young preacher to a place of execution, where Stephen was to die beneath a pile of stones. ". . . and the witnesses laid down their clothes at a young man's feet, whose name was Saul" (Acts 7:58). Luke wrote: "And Saul was consenting unto his (Stephen's) death" (Acts 8:1). The memory of that terrible murder would not die, and Saul's life became a nightmare. His misery deepened, and believing something had to be done to quiet his conscience, ". . . Saul, yet breathing out threatenings and slaughter against the disciples of the Lord, went unto the high priest" (Acts 9:1). Even Ananias, a devout man in Damascus, fearfully exclaimed, "Lord, I have heard by many of this man, how much evil he hath done to thy saints at Jerusalem . . ." (Acts 9:13). But the Lord was pleased — He had found a man to stand in the gap!

The new convert did what Christ had commanded the original disciples — he went into the known world, and did more for world evangelism than the combined efforts of all other church leaders. The apostle never forgot the moment when he heard the Savior's words: "Depart: for I will send you far hence unto the Gentiles" (Acts 22:21). At first he argued with Christ because he desperately desired to evangelize his own nation. Thereafter he never faltered in his mission and after many years triumphantly wrote to Timothy: "For I am now ready to be offered, and the time of my departure is at hand. I have fought a good fight, I have finished my course, I have kept the faith: Henceforth there is laid up for me a crown of righteousness, which the Lord, the righteous judge, shall give me at that day . . ." (2 Tim. 4:6-8).

The Sacred Decision . . . *How Willing*

How can any person describe the indescribable, or express the inexpressible? There was a moment of stillness when the Divine Family considered their greatest project. Far down the corridor of time, they saw a devastated world in which innumerable people needed a friend. Enormous guilt endangered the souls of men, and the outlook was bleak. Perhaps Isaiah was not the first person to hear the words: "Whom shall I send, and who will go for us?" (Isa. 6:8). Then a voice was heard in the eternal stillness: "I will do it—but I will need to become a man."

Paul was aware of that great decision when he wrote: "Let this mind be in you, which was also in Christ Jesus: Who, being in the form of God, thought it not robbery to be equal with God: But made himself of no reputation, and took upon him the form of a servant, and was made in the likeness of men. And being found in fashion as a man, he humbled himself, and became obedient unto death, even the death of the cross" (Phil. 2:5-8). When Mary held her new-born Child, even the angels rejoiced; they knew God had found His Man!

When the Salvation Army was one of the greatest movements on earth, the founder, and First General, was asked to explain his effectiveness as a spiritual leader. General Booth's reply was self-explanatory. He said: "I will tell you the secret. God has had all there was of me. There have been men with greater brains than mine; men with greater opportunities, but from the day I got the poor of London on my heart, and a vision of what Jesus Christ could do for them, I made up my mind that God should have all of William Booth. If anything has been achieved, it is because God had all the adoration of my heart, all the power of my will, and all the influence of my life."

Is God still looking for someone to do a special task? Could He be searching for you, or me?

THE MAN WITH THE
UNWANTED TENANT (MATTHEW 12:43-45)

It is interesting to note that when the writers of the Gospels wrote their memoirs, they only mentioned 27 occasions when people were individually healed by the Savior. Infrequently Jesus performed mass-miracles when He helped all the sufferers in His audience, but, apart from those events, the people healed were few. The 27 instances mentioned suggested Christ delivered fewer than nine every year, or less than one per month. This seems to be astonishing when modern faith-healers claim hundreds of miracles in every service. There must be an explanation for this surprising fact.

Luke described how ten lepers were healed in a moment, but nine went away to disappear into obscurity (Luke 17:12-18). Matthew tells of two demoniacs who were delivered at Gadara, but one was never seen again (Matt. 9:28). The same might be said of one of the two blind men who were given sight in Jericho (Matt. 20:30-34). Luke also mentioned a man who said to the Lord: "I will follow thee—*but* . . ."; apparently he never fulfilled his original vow.

Many people admired Christ, but avoided discipleship. Probably, they considered themselves incapable of emulating His example. Millions of people continue to say: "I would like to become a Christian, but could never live that life."

The Strange Dwelling . . . *Divided*

The Savior was an expert in the art of painting word-pictures, but His description of the haunted house was a masterpiece! When He described the strange conditions prevailing in a hypothetical home, His listeners were able to visualize the strange house in which lived an honest citizen and a demon. One end of the structure was attractive, clean and inviting; the other, filthy, neglected and forbidding. When seen through modern eyes, one half of the building was charmingly decorated, beautifully curtained; its appearance indicated loving and continuing pride. Yet the other was conspicuous for cobwebs and dirty windows. Peeling paint and rags had replaced draperies.

Looking through the window was a demented creature who was determined never to vacate the premises. The householder detested the unwanted neighbor but was too weak to enforce an eviction.

Thus did the Savior describe a human soul in which sincerity longed for what appeared to be unobtainable freedom. That scene vividly described people who said: "We would love to become Christians, but unfortunately, there resides within us enemies we cannot control. If we followed Christ, we might dishonor His name."

The Startling Decision . . . *Demonstrated*

Then, unexpectedly, a miracle happened! A new determination filled the owner of the house, and with increasing courage, he entered the dirty section of the ruined home, and fiercely evicted the demon. Probably he surprised himself—he had accomplished the impossible!

The spring cleaning which followed beggared description. Untiring energy banished filth. New drapes were hung in the repaired windows, and the homestead became what it was meant to be. The songs of the householder echoed throughout the home; he had discovered a happiness thought to be beyond his reach. A new future awaited him; the terrible experience of living with a devil had become a memory; his dreams had come true!

Probably the Savior smiled at His captivated audience. The listeners knew Christ was expressing the conviction that God could deliver men from the power of evil. The idea was marvelous, but surely there was a flaw somewhere! They visualized the householder proudly surveying his reclaimed home, and appreciated the satisfaction shining on his face. Yet, their speculative eyes seemed to be asking: "Will the expelled demon return? Would this happiness be lasting or temporary?" The Lord read their thoughts, and proceeded with His message.

The Saddening Defeat . . . *Disturbing*

The Teacher said: "When the unclean spirit is gone out of a man, he walketh through dry places, seeking rest, and findeth none. Then he saith, I will return into my house from whence I came out; and when he is come, he findeth it empty, swept, and garnished . . ." The Amplified Version translates the text: "Then he says: I will go back to my house from which I came out. And when he arrives, he finds the place unoccupied, swept, put in order, and decorated."

The inference in Christ's remarks was obvious, but it created a problem. The demon knew it would be unwise to return to his former home — alone! He had been expelled once; the householder would evict him again. Evidently help was needed. "Then goeth he, and taketh with himself seven other spirits, more wicked than himself, and they enter in and dwell there: and the last state of that man is worse than the first."

Modern people respond to that detail with an excuse saying: "That is precisely the reason why we do not embrace the doctrines of Christianity. Knowing our weaknesses, we hesitate to embark upon a new way of living lest we fail, and increasing shame would increase our frustration. It is better to tolerate one devil than to run the risk of living with eight!"

The Sublime Deliverer . . . *Defending*

Evidently, there was a flaw in the parable. The householder, having expelled his evil companion, made a mistake—*he decided to live alone*! When the evil spirit returned, he found the residence *empty*. The owner, pleased with his achievement, had left the place unguarded, and during his absence the undesirable tenant returned to make new plans.

No one can maintain a ceaseless watch; every man needs to sleep! The reason for the ensuing failure was that the house remained unguarded. If the householder had enjoyed the companionship of a guest with similar desires and ambitions, they could have shared the responsibility of protecting their house. However, the new friend would need the power to overcome devils.

This scripture can only be understood when considered in its context. Christ had already demonstrated His ability to expel demons. The evil spirits within the maniac from Gadara confessed they were legion; that is, they were six thousand in number, and any person capable of overcoming that kind of opposition would have no problem expelling eight enemies (Luke 8:30). Matthew described how a demoniac was delivered by Christ, and the reality of the miracle was never denied by the Pharisees. Accepting the fact, they tried to explain it by claiming Jesus collaborated with Beelzebub the chief of demons.

It would appear, therefore, that the secret of the householder's triumph would have been an invitation to Christ to accept hospitality. The Lord could, and would, enable men to triumph in all circumstances of life. Paul expounded these truths throughout his epistles.

A. The Unclean House

The apostle wrote: "For I know that in me (that is, in my flesh) dwelleth no good thing: for to will is present with me; but how to perform that which is good I find not. For the good that I would, I do not; but the evil which I would not, that I do. Now if I do that I would not, it is no more I that do it, but sin that dwelleth in me" (Rom. 7:18-20). Paul and wickedness lived in the same house!

B. The Unprecedented Hope

"To whom God would make known what is the riches of the glory of this mystery among the Gentiles; which is *Christ in you the hope of glory*" (Col. 1:27). That statement expressed the greatest truth in the Gospel message. It was, and still is, inconceivable to unbelievers that anyone who had died could still be alive and able to reside within his followers. Yet Paul insisted that Christ could be formed within redeemed souls, and by the power of the indwelling Spirit, He could enrich the lives of God's children. Christians should invite Him to share their dwelling, and gain victory over the evil which might already be there.

C. The Unending Companionship

Paul said, "I can do all things through Christ which strengtheneth me" (Phil. 4:13). The Lord left His disciples so that in another form He could remain with them forever. Throughout

His earthly ministry the Savior was restricted by physical limitations. He could not be in Jerusalem and Capernaum at the same moment! He said: "Nevertheless I tell you the truth; It is expedient for you that I go away: for if I go not away, the Comforter will not come unto you; but if I depart, I will send him unto you" (John 16:7).

Speaking of the Lord, Paul said: "And he said unto me, My grace is sufficient for thee; for my strength is made perfect in weakness . . ." (2 Cor. 12:9). Christ not only cleanses the human temple; He enables the believer to maintain its purity.

During my stay in Australia, I met a remarkable man who had served several years in a prison. He told me that as far back as he could remember he had been a kleptomaniac. Even when he was a young boy he constantly felt an irrepressible urge to steal. His criminal deeds ruined his life. Then one day he became a Christian and everything changed. I listened to his testimony and saw intense gratitude shining in his eyes. When I asked, "Do you ever feel an urge to steal now?", he paused for several moments before replying: "Yes, Sir, there are times when the old urge comes over me like a flood. That feeling is terrible." I continued: "When that happens, what do you do?" As tears filled his eyes, he said: "Sir, I look to Jesus, and He holds me fast."

THE BEST PLACE IN THE
WORLD . . . at the feet of Jesus   (MATTHEW 15:30)

"The eye of the needle" was the small gate built into the large gates of Jerusalem. Probably, the Lord had seen a cameleer striving desperately to squeeze his camel through the narrow opening. First, all the baggage had to be removed; then the animal was commanded to kneel and be persuaded to pass through the small aperture. It was a difficult and complicated maneuver, but a determined traveler often accomplished the challenging task. Every listener understood what Christ meant when He said: ". . . It is easier for a camel to go through the eye of a needle, than for a rich man to enter into the kingdom of God" (Matt. 19:24).

Proud citizens refused to kneel before Christ. It was almost impossible for them to off-load their treasures and advance on their knees into the kingdom of God! That, apparently, was an art few people acquired. Men are tallest when they kneel at the feet of the Savior. Certain texts considered together provide an interesting progression of thought.

Peter Fell Down . . . *The Place of Conviction* (Luke 5:8)

Simon Peter never forgot the morning when the Savior walked toward him on the beach of the Sea of Galilee. With increasing interest he watched the approaching crowd, but when the Stranger stepped into the empty boat, took a seat, and asked Peter to row the boat away from the shore, he probably smiled and did as Jesus had asked. It was the first time his fishing boat had been used as a pulpit.

It is not known whether or not he attended the synagogue services; perhaps his occupation left little time for religious activities. That morning Peter heard the greatest sermon he had ever heard. Its content has never been disclosed, but it may be safely assumed, as it continued, Simon became increasingly agitated. The writers of the Gospels never revealed how long Jesus spoke, but when the unique seaside service terminated, Simon was asked to go to deeper water and prepare to catch fish.

Peter's admiration for the Preacher was never in doubt, but what had been requested seemed foolish since the fishermen had worked all the night without success. Nevertheless, he had no desire to displease the Stranger, so he replied: "Master, we have toiled all the night, and have taken nothing: nevertheless at thy word I will let down the net" (Luke 5:5). Peter committed an expensive mistake. He was told to let down his *nets*. The fish which should have been in two, three or four nets, went into the one which immediately commenced to break. "When Simon Peter saw it, he fell down at Jesus' knees, saying, Depart from me; for I am a sinful man, O Lord."

It is important to remember Peter caught the fish *after* he had heard the Savior's sermon. To use the proverbial saying: "It was the last straw which broke the camel's back!" Probably Simon was seated behind the Lord, but as he skillfully handled the boat, Christ's message convicted him. He remembered things he had done and said, and guilt overwhelmed his soul as he said: "Depart from me, for I am a sinful man, O Lord." It is impossible to hear the Gospel of Christ without being troubled by a sense of unworthiness.

Zacchaeus Came Down . . . *The Place of Contrition*
(Luke 19:6)

The story of Zacchaeus is one of the most intriguing in the New Testament. It was written: "He sought to see Jesus *who he was*. . . ." It appears to be incomprehensible that after three and a half years of Christ's amazing ministry, there remained a man unaware of the identity and personality of Jesus of Nazareth. (1) Was the tax-gatherer so isolated from his fellow Jews that he had remained ignorant of events within the nation? (2) Was this an unusual commotion in Jericho when, unexpectedly, people thronged the streets? Did Zacchaeus emerge from his office asking, "What is the cause of this disturbance?" Maybe he had heard about the miracle-worker from Nazareth, and hearing He was near, became anxious to see Him. He was very diminutive, and to gain a better view, climbed into a sycamore tree. The low-lying branches enabled him to find a suitable vantage point.

Zacchaeus was the chief tax-gatherer in Jericho, and it is

believed his position was exploited to increase personal wealth. Perhaps, unlike Peter, he was self-righteous. Curiosity helped him climb the tree, but concern brought him back to the street. Zacchaeus, who had never heard the Savior, looked into the Lord's face, and heard: "Zacchaeus, make haste, and come down; for today I must abide at thy house." He was detested by the Pharisees, but their contempt was meaningless. He realized that Jesus knew him, loved him, and desired a welcome into his home.

It may be significant that the man did not say: "Lord, the half of my goods *I will* give to the poor; and if I have taken anything from any man by false accusation *I will* restore him fourfold." It would appear from the text that this had already been his common practice; that he was fair, honorable and just. That may or may not have been the case, but at least it may be said his testimony would be attractive to people who advertise their personal virtue. The view from the feet of Jesus is infinitely better than any seen from a tree!

The Palsied Man Was Let Down . . . *The Place of Conversion* (Luke 5:19)

Blessed is the man whose friends desire to bring him to Christ. "And behold, men brought in a bed a man which was taken with a palsy: and they sought means to bring him in, and to lay him before him. And when they could not find by what way they might bring him in because of the multitude, they went upon the housetop, and let him down through the tiling with his couch into the midst before Jesus." Webster's Dictionary describes palsy as being: "paralysis of any part of the body sometimes accompanied with involuntary tremors." The shaking palsy was "A chronic degenerative disease of the central nervous system characterized by tremors, muscular rigidity, weakness, and a masklike expression." His condition and experience can be summarized under four headings.

(1) *He was sick.* His disease had reached vital parts of his body; he had become helpless and hopeless; there was no known cure for his ailment. Jesus said the cause of his condition was sin, but, apparently, the sufferer was either ignorant of that fact, or had forgotten it.

(2) *He was sure.* Carried by four of his friends, the man approached the building in which Jesus was speaking, but the size of the audience made a normal entry impossible. Undaunted, his carriers ascended steps to the roof to remove the tiles. The owner of the building would become annoyed that his property had been damaged, but the sick man believed he would be able to assume responsibility for repairs.

(3) *He was surprised.* When the Lord said: "Man, thy sins are forgiven thee," the most amazed man in the place was the suppliant. He had not come seeking forgiveness, but to be healed! Yet, Jesus affirmed the cause of his ailment was previously committed sin. Having dealt with the cause of the trouble, it became easy for Christ to remove its effect.

(4) *He was saved.* The man's life was transformed; his pain was replaced by peace; paralysis by praise; helplessness by happiness. Everything changed when he reached the feet of Jesus.

The Father Kneeled Down . . . *The Place of Concern*
(Matt. 17:14)

"And when they were come to the multitude, there came to him a certain man, kneeling down to him, and saying, Lord have mercy on my son: for he is a lunatic and sore vexed: for ofttimes he falleth into the fire, and oft into the water. And I brought him to thy disciples, and they could not cure him" (Matt. 17:14-16).

The father was desperate; he had exhausted his resources. Every person in the community believed his son was possessed by a demon, and avoided contact with the family. The lad needed constant attention and it was recognized his unpredictable actions could cause death.

Apparently, the grieving parent had no physical ailments, but his boy's condition was heart-breaking. He yearned for the lad's deliverance, and this became evident when he knelt with uplifted arms before Christ. The man had overcome doubt and disappointment, for while Jesus had been on the Mount of Transfiguration, his boy had been brought to the disciples. Those self-confident men laid their hands on the stricken child; they failed to expel the demon. It would be difficult to describe the disappointment of the father who expected much, but received nothing. Nevertheless, he was not without hope; his faith was centered in Christ. Followers of Christ may fail ignominiously, but the Savior continues to perform the impossible. He succeeds when all others fail.

Mary Sat Down . . . *The Place of Contentment* (Luke 10:39)

"Now it came to pass, as they went, that Jesus entered into a certain village: and a certain woman named Martha received him into her house. And she had a sister called Mary, which also sat at Jesus' feet, and heard his word" (Luke 10:38-39). The devoted family in Bethany provided interesting contrasts. Lazarus, the head of the household, was not an aggressive character. Apart from his being raised from the dead, little would be known about him. He was quiet, dependable and loyal. When his sisters asked Jesus for assistance, they said: "Lord, behold he whom thou lovest is sick" (John 11:3). Martha was the leader in the family; she made the decisions, and apparently was never challenged. She invited the Lord to enter her home. Martha usually completed a task before others could begin!

Mary was contemplative, a dreamer, who traveled far while sitting still! She looked into the eyes of Jesus and saw the heart of God! Martha was *industrious*; Lazarus was *illustrious*; but Mary was *inspired*. She was not an invaluable helper when work needed to be done. The duties of the kitchen were unattractive when Jesus was speaking in the sitting room! The bread in the oven was forgotten when manna from heaven was falling in the next room! She sat at the feet of Jesus — and was content.

(1) *Her Increasing Desire to Learn.* When other people discussed the miracles of Jesus, Mary considered His message. What He said was more attractive than anything He did. Had she been given the choice of being present in an amazing healing service or sitting quietly in His Bible class, her choice would have been immediate. She was a most attentive listener, for everything He said was of the utmost importance. She was His most ardent disciple; to sit at His feet was heaven!

79

(2) *Her Illuminating Discernment Through Listening.* Her eyes were filled with wonder. She sat in the home of Simon the leper, but her thoughts were elsewhere. Some of the disciples were discussing the expected kingdom, and their enthusiasm was contagious. Yet, Mary frowned. Those men were misinformed — her Lord was about to die. Her eyes were misty; the only kingdom that mattered was that which He intended to establish within the hearts of people who loved Him. He would be the corn of wheat which would die to produce a great harvest. The men listened, but heard nothing! When she anointed the Lord with her valuable ointment, onlookers criticized her, but Jesus said: "Let her alone: against the day of my burying hath she kept this" (see John 12:7).

(3) *Her Inspired Devotion in Loving.* When she anointed His body, she gave the greatest of all her possessions. There was not much time left; if she intended to give Him a special gift, there was need for haste. Nothing was too good for her Lord. When Martha complained about Mary's absence from the kitchen, Jesus replied: "Martha, Martha, thou art careful and troubled about many things: But one thing is needful: and Mary hath chosen that good part, which shall not be taken away from her" (Luke 10:41-42). Faithful service is excellent, but unless continuing and deepening love for Christ be its inspiration, delight becomes a drudgery, and the joy of Christian living a memory.

This was the most informative of the parables of the Savior. No other speaker said so much in such few words. Christ's story reached from everlasting to everlasting; it embraced eternity, and its significance never diminished. It may be impossible to decide the exact age of our planet, but the first humans were created approximately 6,000 years ago. The Bible teaches that before the end of time, the Lord will reign for 1,000 years, and therefore it may be concluded that man's existence upon the earth will continue for at least 7,000 years. Eternal ages preceded the creation of the first humans, and will continue after the cessation of time. It was truly remarkable that the parable given by Jesus included everything to be revealed between those two extremes.

The Scriptures were written by many authors over great periods of time, and in various locations. They began with the ages preceding creation and conclude with events to take place after the close of human history. Biblical authors told their story in 66 books divided into 41,173 verses. It was remarkable that Jesus only needed twelve verses to describe God's plan for all ages. The Savior said in two minutes what prophets and scribes told and wrote over a period of 4,000 years. This wonderful piece of oratory should be an example for all long-winded preachers!

God's Supreme Purpose . . . *To Celebrate the Marriage of His Son*

Paul, whose insight into the eternal purposes of God exceeded anything possessed by other apostles, wrote to the Ephesians declaring that God "Having made known unto us the mystery of his will, according to his good pleasure which he hath purposed in himself; That in the dispensation of the fullness of times he might gather together in one all things in Christ, both which are in heaven, and which are on earth, even in him . . ." (Eph. 1:9-10). Before the beginning of history God planned what would be accomplished before the end of time. For example, Paul said: ". . . he hath chosen us in him *before the founda-*

tion of the world . . ." (Eph. 1:4). John wrote: ". . . in the book of life of *the Lamb slain from the foundation of the world*" (Rev. 13:8). Isaiah made an astonishing prediction when he wrote: "For unto us a child is born, unto us a son is given; and the government shall be upon his shoulder; and his name shall be called Wonderful, Counsellor, The mighty God, The everlasting Father, The Prince of Peace. Of the increase of his government and peace there shall be no end, upon the throne of David, and upon his kingdom, to order it, and to establish it with judgment and with justice *from henceforth even forever*. The zeal of the Lord of hosts will perform this" (Isa. 9:6-7).

During the ages preceding time, God planned a glorious celebration to commemorate the occasion when the promised Messiah would establish His everlasting kingdom and nothing can prevent that supreme event. The Lord Jesus Christ, Who was present when the plan was first formulated, expressed that truth in His immortal parable. God's original plan never changed. Wars may come and go; political leaders may rise and fall; but mankind may be assured Paul was correct when he wrote: "That at the name of Jesus every knee should bow, of things in heaven, and things in earth, and things under the earth; And that every tongue should confess that Jesus Christ is Lord, to the glory of God the Father" (Phil. 2:10-11).

God's Strange People . . . *Who Ignored a Great Invitation*

". . . a certain king . . . sent forth his servants to call them that were bidden to the wedding: *and they would not come.* Again, he sent forth other servants, saying, Behold, I have prepared my dinner; my oxen and my fatlings are killed, and all things are ready: come unto the marriage. But *they made light of it*, and went their ways, one to his farm, another to his merchandise: And the remnant took his servants, and entreated them spitefully, and slew them" (Matt. 22:3-6). It should be remembered that when Jesus told this parable, Christian martyrs had not died for their faith, and therefore the Lord's message was an indictment against the Jews who had spurned God's message, and killed some of His messengers. Luke, in recording this parable, did not mention the avenging armies of the offended monarch. If Matthew wrote his Gospel after the destruction of the temple in 70 A.D. he may have believed the calamity was the fulfillment of the prediction made in the parable of the king's supper.

The two statements *"they would not come"* and *"they made light of it,"* provided eloquent testimony to the indifference of the invited guests. They decided not to respond to the king's invitation, and were indifferent to future consequences. Luke was more explicit in describing the refusal to attend the supper. He wrote: "And they all with one accord began to make excuse. The first said unto him, I have bought a piece of ground, and must needs go and see it: I pray thee have me excused." The purchased land would not disappear overnight, and could be seen at any other time. Jesus said: "For where your treasure is, there will your heart be also" (Matt. 6:21). Evidently the man thought more of his new property than he did of its Creator.

"And another said, I have bought five yoke of oxen, and I go to prove them: I pray thee have me excused." Apparently the farmer had already purchased extra animals to pull his plows. Now he wanted to know whether they would be capable of doing their job. His reasoning was without merit, for if he bought oxen without knowledge of their health and strength, he was a very foolish man. "And another said, I have married a wife, and therefore I cannot come." This statement was the most ludicrous of the three. Women seldom exercised authority during the time when the Lord was upon the earth. Any man who desired the company of a new wife would have remained with her during the honeymoon. The three men mentioned in the Lord's parable were only concerned about material matters, and disliked interference in their private concerns.

When Jesus described the attacks made upon the messengers, He referred to the Hebrew fathers who persecuted and killed God's prophets. The people were not only indifferent to the entreaties of the monarch; they disliked the supper even though it was provided by a king! It has often been said one never misses the water until the well runs dry! Israel never realized the folly of idolatry until they saw it in Babylon. Jeremiah said: "For my people have committed two evils; they have forsaken me, the fountain of living waters, and hewed them out cisterns, broken cisterns, that can hold no water" (Jer. 2:13).

God's Surprising Plan . . . *To Invite Gentiles*

"Then said he (the king) to his servants, The wedding is ready, but they which were bidden were not worthy. Go ye therefore into the highways, and as many as ye shall find, bid to the marriage. So those servants went out into the highways, and gathered together all as many as they found, both bad and good; and the wedding was furnished with guests" (Matt. 22:8-10).

The apostle Paul clearly understood this message. Writing to the Christians in Ephesus, he said: "That at that time ye were without Christ, being aliens from the commonwealth of Israel, and strangers from the covenants of promise, having no hope, and without God in the world" (Eph. 2:12). The converts in Ephesus were Gentiles, and yet *to them* Paul wrote: ". . . he hath chosen *us* in him before the foundation of the world . . ." (Eph. 1:4).

It was difficult for orthodox Jews to understand this fact, for throughout their long history, fellowship with pagan nations had been prohibited. To preserve the integrity of His people, God commanded them to be separated from the customs of heathens, and marriage with other nations was strictly forbidden. Following these principles, the Hebrews became an isolated people who considered themselves superior to other races. Jehovah was their God; Gentiles were considered to be dogs (Matt. 15:26). Many of the Christians in Rome were also Gentiles, but to them Paul wrote: "And *we* know that all things work together for good to them that love God, to them who are the called according to his purpose. For whom he did foreknow, he also did predestinate to be conformed to the image of his Son, that he might be the firstborn among many brethren" (Rom. 8:28-29). This was the great mystery hidden in the mind of God, and revealed to Paul that he might proclaim it to all nations.

God's Stupendous Provision . . . *To Supply Wedding Garments*

Everything necessary for this wedding was supplied by the

king. Pastor James Smith admirably expressed this fact when he wrote: "Those who came to this feast found what sinners find on coming to Christ. (1) *Rest on a princely couch.* (2) *Shelter under a princely roof.* (3) *Satisfaction at a princely table.* (4) *Fellowship with princely friends*" (quoted from *Handsful on Purpose, series 1,* pg. 182, published by the William B. Eerdmans Publishing Company, Grand Rapids, Michigan). The Savior said: "A certain king made a marriage for his son." The same monarch issued all the invitations and spoke of "my dinner; my oxen and my fatlings." Furthermore, at all eastern weddings of this magnitude, each guest was supplied with a wedding garment which was a gift from the king. The details of the wedding reception were carefully planned so that the entire scene would be spectacularly beautiful. There were no conflicting colors; everything harmonized with the surroundings, and nothing was permitted to spoil the resplendent celebration.

The Savior deliberately described the preparations for the wedding, for they were to be illustrative of things planned in heaven. He indicated that clothing would be an essential part of heaven's greatest occasion. Each person at the Marriage Supper of the Lamb will be clothed in fine linen, which is the righteousness of the saints. John wrote: "Let us be glad and rejoice, and give honor to him, for the marriage of the Lamb is come, and his wife hath made herself ready. And to her was granted that she should be arrayed in fine linen, clean and white: for the fine linen is the righteousness of saints" (Rev. 19:7-8). The Bible also speaks of (1) *The garments of salvation and the robe of righteousness* (Isa. 61:10); (2) *The garment of holiness* (Exod. 31:10); (3) *The garment of humility* (1 Peter 5:5) and (4) *The garment of praise* (Isa. 61:3). The same truth was expressed when the Lord clothed the demoniac of Gadara. Guests at a wedding were not admitted because they were clothed in their own expensive attire, nor were they excluded because they were clad in rags. The king freely supplied the necessary garments, and the right of admission was guaranteed to the individual when he accepted the offered gift.

God's Startling Perception . . . *"The king . . . saw a man!"*

"And when the king came in to see the guests, he saw there a

85

man which had not on a wedding garment: And he saith unto him, Friend, how camest thou in hither not having a wedding garment? And he was speechless." Entrance to the banquet hall in a palace could only be made through a doorway. Jesus described how the assembled guests came from the highways and byways; they were good and bad; ordinary citizens and derelicts. They received the invitation and came just as they were. Many of them had no homes in which to prepare for the celebrated occasion; they could only wash their faces, hands and feet. If they were beggars, they had no spare clothing, and did not object to the exchange of rags for resplendence. Yet one man, for reasons not known, preferred to reject the king's garment; evidently he was satisfied with his appearance. He refused the offer made by the servant of the king, and proudly entered believing he was admirable. He spurned a royal offer, disregarded the cost of the garment, and unwisely proclaimed he was self-sufficient.

Unfortunately, that type of person still exists. When Paul wrote to the Ephesians, he said: "For by grace are ye saved through faith; and that not of yourselves it is the gift of God. Not of works, lest any man should boast" (Eph. 2:8-9). To provide sinners with garments of salvation God gave His Son, Who offered His precious blood as a ransom for many. Peter, in his sermon at Pentecost, declared only Jesus could provide salvation (Acts 4:12). Men who rely upon their own righteousness are too blind to see, and too unwise to understand the message of Christ.

God's Solemn Pronouncement . . . *"Take him away"*

"Then said the king to the servants, Bind him hand and foot, and take him away, and cast him into outer darkness; there shall be weeping and gnashing of teeth. For many are called, but few are chosen." The king's decision was final. Jesus meant this to be a warning that the judgment of God would fall upon all people who rejected the offer of eternal salvation. Suggestions that people can never be lost eternally are not based on the Word of God. The writer to the Hebrews stated: ". . . it is appointed unto men once to die, but after this the judgment"

(Heb. 9:27). People who reject God's offer on earth will never receive His blessing in eternity. It is frightening to consider the things from which the offender was led away.

He was led away from the fellowship of accepted guests. This was replaced by eternal loneliness. *He lost the opportunity of hearing inspiring testimonies.* This possibility gave place to weeping and gnashing of teeth. *The man lost the privilege of attending the marriage and seeing the faces of the Royal Couple.* He never shared in the joy of the marriage; it was exchanged for eternal sorrow and bitter memories of his earlier stupidity.

Thus did Jesus explain His final commission. He said: "Go ye therefore, and teach all nations, Baptizing them in the name of the Father, and of the Son, and of the Holy Ghost: Teaching them to observe all things whatsoever I have commanded you . . ." (Matt. 28:20).

Centuries have passed since Christ gave to His disciples that great task, and unfortunately many things have changed within the modern world. Some preachers have either forgotten or rejected what Christ said. He taught that the wedding garment was purchased and provided by God. Modern thinkers believe virtue and sincere endeavor are acceptable substitutes for the reconciling death of Jesus. It is believed that when a man does his best, even God cannot expect more. Advocates of international religions teach there are many ways by which to reach heaven. Buddhists, Moslems and other nations reject the teaching of Jesus. If their views be correct, then Christ was wrong when He said: ". . . I am the way, the truth, and the life: *no man cometh unto the Father, but by me*" (John 14:6, italics mine).

If there be any other way of reaching heaven, Jesus would have said so. If non-Christians who are religious will safely reach their goal, then the Christian Church was absurd in sending missionaries to places where they were not needed! Unfortunately, heathen philosophy has diluted our faith and paralyzed our efforts. The Savior believed God would offer salvation to unworthy sinners; that destiny would be decided when people either accepted or rejected His provision. He evidently believed that men who relied entirely upon their own righteousness would be condemned. He also encouraged evangelism and instructed His servants to go into the highways and byways of the world to persuade listeners to accept the good news, and come as they were to the marriage. Liberal preachers would be more effective if they sat at the feet of Jesus and listened! It should never be forgotten that God said: ". . . This is my beloved Son, in whom I am well pleased; *hear ye Him*" (Matt. 17:5).

Some time after the conclusion of World War I, a remarkable event took place in the theater of a cruise ship. The entertainment center was crowded with appreciative people when one of the passengers walked to the stage to sing. The listeners expected to hear a popular melody, but instead heard "Jesus Lover of my Soul, Let me to Thy bosom fly." As the wonderful baritone voice filled the theater, the audience was spellbound. The soloist possessed a rare voice, and his singing of the hymn was electrifying.

One of the listeners was very thoughtful; the rendering had stirred memories. Approaching the singer, he asked: "Sir, were you in the war?" When the answer was given in the affirmative, he continued, "Were you with a certain regiment?" and the name was given. Astonished the singer answered: "Yes, I was, but how did you know?"

The two men sat at a table and reminisced. The questioner was a German who said: "On that particular night I, with others, was ordered to reconnoiter the enemy's position, and my assignment was to kill the sentry. We crawled through the darkness, and finally, I was very close to my objective. Unless I am mistaken, you were the man. Suddenly, you began to sing softly the hymn you sang tonight, and I knew you were a Christian. I returned to the German trenches to tell my officer it would be foolish to attack; the British had received reinforcements. Our plans were then changed."

The singer thought for a moment and then replied: "Yes, I remember that night very well. When I was posted to a dangerous position as a sentry I was apprehensive and believed I was about to die. There in the darkness I began to sing, for I knew only the Savior could help me."

The German replied: "Friend, that hymn saved your life."

Music is a God-given gift, but when a man sings in adversity, his action reflects the greatness of his soul. His voice is a window through which may be seen his finer attributes.

This was particularly true of the Lord Jesus Christ. At the close of His final passover, Jesus sang with His disciples. Perhaps the Lord often hummed tunes and sang psalms, but such occurrences were never mentioned in the Gospels. His singing at a time of extreme adversity was astounding and inspiring.

The disciples were bewildered. What was meant to be a joyous occasion had become a time of tension, fear and suspicion. For many years those men had observed the Passover celebration, and their souls had been refreshed with memories and gratitude. At each feast they remembered the miraculous deliverance of the nation from bondage, and reverently partook of the herbs and spices ordained to commemorate that event. Time was meaningless when those worshiping people thoughtfully ate their portion of the lamb, and recalled how the Angel of Death passed through the land of Egypt. Each time they sang the Hallel—the specified psalms of praise—they sang lustily and joyfully; their souls rejoiced in praising God. Passover was always the greatest event in Israel's year.

Nevertheless, the disciples recognized this commemoration left much to be desired. The atmosphere within the upper room was oppressive. The entire proceedings chilled their spirits; they were apprehensive, for treachery within their ranks had been exposed. They were mystified, for although the host had made ample preparation for their passover requirements, the all-important lamb had been neglected. Jesus had substituted Himself, and had spoken of His body and blood. It was confusing.

The ceremony terminated; the time for praise had arrived. But how could broken hearts rejoice, and fearful people sing praises to God? How could they rejoice over an event from antiquity, when their future was ominous? Their silence was unbroken until Jesus announced the famous Hallel, and, with His strong resonant voice, pitched the tune and began to sing. Slowly, uncertainly, the men emulated His example, and years later, remembering that moment, Matthew wrote:

"And when they had sung an hymn, they went out into the mount of Olives."

The Song Which Stirred Memories

To many harassed people, the fact that Jesus sang at such a moment was one of the strangest incidents in the New Testament. The disciples only suspected what might happen, but the Lord knew rejection; a flogging and crucifixion awaited Him. His face would be marred beyond recognition, and even His perspiration would appear as drops of blood falling to the ground. Ordinarily, men would have feared those sufferings, but resolutely the Lord expelled such thoughts, and began to sing the praises of God. That strange, yet glorious, fact defied human understanding.

The Lord and His disciples did not sing a short chorus, or even one psalm. The Hallel included several sonnets. Therefore, it may be concluded the singing continued for ten, fifteen, or even twenty minutes. How the Lord maintained His composure may never be fully understood. It is safe to assume the music that night stirred His heart, for this was a repetition of something done annually; it was a testimony to the faithfulness of God, Who had preserved Israel through extreme adversity.

There is reason to believe the Lord had memorized every word of those psalms. As He sang, the Savior's thoughts encompassed Israel's history. Repeatedly, God's people had been attacked by their enemies; their land had been devastated; crops were destroyed and Jerusalem ransacked. The people had survived many ordeals, the greatest of which was prolonged captivity in Babylon. Yet, God's faithfulness had never faltered, and the existence of the nation during our Lord's sojourn upon earth was evidence of the dependability of Jehovah. He had honored His promises.

When Jesus sang at the Passover, He knew He could safely confront His future, assured of ultimate victory. He could trust His Heavenly Father. Later, when all seemed to be lost, He exclaimed: "Into thy hands I commend my spirit" (Luke 23:46). His faith was completely justified, for "Christ was raised up from the dead by the glory of his Father" (Rom. 6:4). No man nor woman can be wrong trusting God.

Charles Wesley, who lived from 1707 until 1788, wrote 6500 hymns, but his greatest composition was probably the hymn, "Jesus Lover of my soul, Let me to thy bosom fly." It is interesting to know that when this hymn was first offered to his brother John, the great preacher rejected it as being too sentimental, and it was not until after the author's death, the sacred song came into general use among churches.

Henry Ward Beecher, one the greatest American preachers wrote: "I would rather have written that hymn of Wesley's than to have the fame of all the kings that ever sat on earth. I would rather be the author of that hymn than to hold the wealth of the richest man in New York. He will die after a little while, and pass out of men's thoughts. What will there be to speak of him? But people will go on singing Wesley's hymn until the last trump brings forth the angel band; and then, I think, it will mount upon some lips to the very presence of God."

Many stories have suggested incidents which inspired Wesley to write his sonnet. Perhaps the most popular account is that which describes Wesley's frightening experience in a terrible storm while returning from a brief visit to America. When his ship safely reached land, Wesley wrote in his journal for that date, December 3, 1736, "I knelt down and blessed the hand that had conducted me through such inextricable mazes."

It was said that during that storm, a frightened bird flew into the cabin and sheltered itself inside Wesley's coat. The preacher-singer recognized that as the bird found refuge in his bosom, so he had found shelter in God. When he wrote his famous hymn, his soul was singing even before the words were uttered. He was singing in the rain!

The Song Which Stressed Mercy

All commentators, both Jewish and Gentile, agree the Hallel was composed of certain specific psalms which were divided into two categories. Some writers mention *The Great Hallel*, but others describe *the lesser Hallel*. It is impossible to state accurately which was used by the Lord, but that at least is of little importance since both renderings emphasize the same truth. The Pulpit Commentary says: "This was probably the second portion of the Hallel (*Psalms 115-118*) or, if the then ritual was the same as the latter, *Psalm 136*" (Rev. A. Lukyn Williams, M.A., *The Pulpit Commentary*, "Matthew," pg. 524).

One of the most important statements in the first collection of sonnets was "*The LORD hath been mindful of us.*" This evidently referred to many events in the history of the nation, but primarily to the deliverance from the Egyptians. The reaction to the kindness of Jehovah was an intense desire to praise Him. "What shall I render unto the Lord for all his benefits towards me? . . . I will offer to thee the sacrifice of thanksgiving, and will call upon the name of the Lord" (Pss. 115:12 and 116:12,17). The first section of the famous Hallel was comprised of 68 of our verses; the second only had 26, and in all probability was favored by worshipers.

It is interesting to note the psalmist, in every verse of his sonnet, repeated a statement—*"for his mercy endureth forever."* Twenty-six times in twenty-six verses the writer used this sentence — obviously, he was trying to emphasize something! The mercy of Jehovah had delivered Israel from Egypt, and His kindness had continued throughout the centuries.

The message of the Psalmist had a profound effect upon the Savior, for He knew the same mercy would soon be extended to the entire world. He realized that all nations were slaves in the bondage of sin and Satan, but God intended to deliver His people in an unprecedented manner. This knowledge was as a rising run before which the shadows of night vanished. Alas, many modern Christians sing hymns without giving attention to the words being sung; Jesus considered what He sang, and rejoiced.

It might be wise to consider the truth expressed by the writer to the Hebrews when he wrote: "Who for *the joy that was set before him*, endured the cross . . ." (Heb. 12:2). The heart of Christ was great enough to welcome the world, and His vision to encompass it. The Lord saw the thief, Saul of Tarsus, and an innumerable host destined to find happiness through His reconciling death. Even the thought of providing an opportunity of salvation to perishing men and women filled the Lord with ecstasy. The Savior knew mercy received led to delight; mercy rejected led to doom. He could not guarantee that every person would accept what was offered, but was determined all people should have an opportunity to become recipients of God's abundant mercy.

Many years ago, the people in the small Welsh community

in which I lived were shocked by a great tragedy. A well-known citizen, in a fit of unprecedented anger, shot his three children. He had looked into a bar to see his wife drinking with other men, and that unfortunate incident led to murder. He was convicted and sent to prison.

I shall always remember a night when I attended an evangelistic service in the local Methodist church. Another man, a notorious drunkard, had been converted in a Salvation Army meeting, and, desiring to tell his friend—the murderer—the good news, went to the prison. He described what had taken place. He was not permitted to enter the cell, but was allowed to speak through the small opening in the door. He said: "I looked through the bars to see my friend, and said: 'Bill, I have to tell you some good news! I have been saved, but I want you to see something for yourself.' He continued, 'I held up my Bible to the bars so that he could read John 3:16, and as he did, he groaned and said, 'That is what I need!'"

If we multiply that incident a millionfold, and then realize how Christ thought of every individual who would find peace through believing, it will not be difficult to appreciate why Jesus sang so enthusiastically at the close of the Passover feast.

The Song with Specific Meaning

Psalm 136 is unique in that it emphasizes three major facts: (1) *The Majesty of God*; (2) *The Mercy of God*; (3) *The Mission of God*. The eyes of the Savior became pools of delight when He sang, for He knew the truths were as relevant to His generation as they had been throughout the history of Israel. As His gaze swept down the corridors of time, He was thrilled that His Father intended to extend mercy to all generations; salvation would be known by millions of people who would hear and believe the Gospel.

1. *The Majesty of God*

Some of the psalmist's statements were exquisite word-pictures. For example, he wrote: "To him that by wisdom made the heavens." "To him that smote Egypt in their firstborn . . . And brought out Israel from among them." "And slew famous kings. . . . And gave their land for an heritage." "Who remembered us in our low estate. . . . And hath redeemed us from our enemies." "O give thanks unto the God of gods." The psalmist insisted God was on His throne far above all principalities and powers, and that every good and perfect gift came from Him (James 1:17).

2. *The Mercy of God*

Evidently, the ancient writer was overwhelmed by the compassion of Jehovah. It seemed incomprehensible that the Ruler of the Universe should be involved with undeserving humans. "He remembered us in our low estate" (Ps. 136:23). Apparently, when this psalm was written, the writer could not forget that God's mercy extended to all people. No man could appreciate that fact more than Jesus.

Paul wrote to the Christians at Philippi: "Let this mind be in you which was also in Christ Jesus: Who, being in the form of God thought it not robbery to be equal with God (that is, divinity was not something to be coveted as was the case when Lucifer fell from heaven). But made himself of no reputation, and took upon him the form of a servant, and was made in the likeness of men. And being found in fashion as a man, he humbled himself, and became obedient unto death, even the death of the cross" (Phil. 2:6-8). When the Savior considered the events of history, and compared them with future events, He knew the mercies of His Father were limitless.

3. *The Mission of God*

Perhaps this was the most important of all revealed facts. Psalm 136 verses 23-25 mentioned three wonderful truths: *He remembered*, *redeemed*, and *refreshed* us. At the precise moment when Christ sang, only He understood the full significance of the words being sung. God had foreseen the needs of mankind when He sent the Lord to live among men. Jehovah had planned eternal redemption through the sacrifice of His Son — the Lamb of God was destined to remove the sin of the world. Redeemed people would become the temple of the Holy Spirit, and God had promised: "No good thing will he withhold from those who walk uprightly." The mission of God was to rescue humanity and bring souls to an eternal home. The fact that Jesus was to be the Agent through which millions of people would find eternal happiness added zest to the Master's singing.

Probably the best loved, and most appreciated American poetess was Miss Fanny Crosby, who was born blind. She possessed the marvelous capacity for singing in the rain! Even from childhood it became obvious that God had compensated her for the absence of eyesight, and even at the early age of eight years, she wrote:

> Oh, what a happy soul am I
> Although I cannot see.
> I am resolved that in this world
> Contented I will be.
>
> How many blessings I enjoy
> That other people don't;
> To weep and sigh because I'm blind
> I cannot and I won't.

On one occasion a well known clergyman said to her: "I think it is a great pity that the Master, when He showered so many gifts upon you, did not give you sight." Her instantaneous reply was: "Do you know that if at birth I had been able to make one petition to my Creator, it would have been that I should have been born blind?" The minister asked: "Why?" Miss Crosby said: "Because when I get to heaven, the first face that shall ever gladden my sight will be that of my Savior." That astonishing but thrilling answer revealed she was an expert at singing in the rain!

The Song Which Silenced Murmuring

The Savior never questioned His Father's plans. Ordinary people would have avoided unprecedented suffering, but the Lord welcomed the inevitable. The writer to the Hebrews said: "Who for the joy that was set before him, endured the cross, despising the shame, and is set down at the right hand of the throne of God" (Heb. 12:2). When the Lord led the singing on that memorable night, His song of praise expressed anticipatory triumph. His soul was thrilled; his faith resplendent. When others might have sought seclusion in which to complain, weep and indulge in self-pity, Jesus triumphantly led His followers in an anthem of immortal praise. The Lord never feared the Cross—He welcomed it!

His victory was shared by some of His disciples. When Paul and Silas were incarcerated in the prison at Philippi, their backs were lacerated, their pain intense, and their future apparently hopeless. Yet . . . "at night Paul and Silas prayed, and sang praises unto God: and the prisoners heard them." This did not take place during a festive occasion; they sang in the storm!

It is thought-provoking to read and compare the singing of Christ at the Passover, and the disciples within the prison. The Master and His men were as trees confronting a storm. Their roots went deep into the promises of God; their leaves transformed the blasts of the hurricane into vibrant music. This is the essence of Christianity; only resilient faith can produce such harmony.

THE STRANGE COMMANDS
OF JESUS (Mark 5:43; 7:36; 8:26)

Personal testimony has always been the spearhead of Christian influence. The church was established upon earth because men and women witnessed about the Savior. "Go home and tell" has been the duty of every Christian. It seems strange, therefore, to discover occasions when the Lord commanded His followers to remain silent. There must have been reasons why He instructed the disciples to refrain from spreading the good news of the Gospel.

Jairus, the Ruler of the Synagogue . . . *How Considerate* (Mark 5:38-43)

"And Jesus charged them straitly *that no man should know it.*" The ruler of the synagogue was confronted by two problems. (1) His daughter was dying, and only Jesus of Nazareth could prevent that tragedy. If the anxious father sought the help of the Savior, serious repercussions would follow. As a leader of the religious community, he had probably warned his people of the dangers of listening to Jesus, Who was believed to be a blasphemer. Jairus was a guardian of the faith, and any man who claimed equality with Jehovah was a menace to the doctrines of the fathers. (2) If he did not seek the assistance of Jesus, he would attend the funeral of his child. If he asked Christ to help, he would become the object of derision and scorn, and would be remembered as a hypocrite who did what he had previously condemned.

That anxious parent was aware of the watchful eyes of his neighbors, but the life of his daughter was at stake. Despair and pride fought within his soul. Should he permit his girl or his pride to die? That was the most momentous decision he would ever make, but the end was never in doubt. "And, behold, there cometh one of the rulers of the synagogue, Jairus by name; and when he saw him he fell at his feet. And besought him greatly, saying, My little daughter lieth at the point of death: I pray thee, come and lay thy hands on her, that she may be healed; and she shall live." The Lord could have healed the child instantly, but instead He "went with him; and much people followed him, and thronged him . . ." (Mark 5:24).

An unexpected delay along the street and the depressing news that the girl had died increased the desperation of the worried ruler. The Lord said: "Be not afraid: only believe." Slowly, they walked along the crowded street, but even before they arrived, the wailing of the professional mourners could be heard. Jesus asked: "Why make ye this ado, and weep? the damsel is not dead but sleepeth. And they laughed him to scorn."

Their pseudo-grief was replaced by sneering laughter; the Teacher was mad! The Lord made them leave the room, and what followed beggared description. The child was restored to life, and a grateful ruler hardly knew how to thank his Benefactor.

The chamber of gloom became a place of gladness, but even the adoring Jairus was surprised when Jesus ". . . charged them straitly that no man should know it . . ." *The Amplified New Testament* renders the text: "He strictly charged them—He commanded them." The Lord was very firm in His remarks. Under no circumstances were they to broadcast the news of the daughter's miraculous recovery. The Savior had reasons for issuing His command.

Was He surrounding Jairus with loving kindness? Angry Jews would criticize the action of their leader, and try to remove him from his position of authority within the community. Instead of the miracle bringing glory to God, it could become the center of a continuing controversy, in which even the daughter might be threatened. At a later time when Jesus raised Lazarus from the dead, the anger of the Lord's enemies was unprecedented. John wrote: "Much people of the Jews therefore knew that he was there: and they came not for Jesus' sake only, but that they might see Lazarus also, whom he had raised from the dead. *But the chief priests consulted that they might put Lazarus also to death; Because that by reason of him many of the Jews went away, and believed on Jesus*" (John 12:9-11).

The Deaf Man with an Impediment . . . *How Challenging*
   (Mark 7:32-36)

"And they bring unto him one that was deaf and had an

impediment in his speech; and they beseech him (Jesus) to put his hand upon him." This was the only miracle of its type mentioned in the scripture. Modern science has created techniques where, in special clinics, deaf people are taught to speak with amazing clarity. When Jesus was upon the earth such facilities were unknown. Deaf people had no way by which to recognize and reproduce sounds, and consequently their speech was indistinct and confusing. Sensitive persons were embarrassed by such an infirmity and probably had this man been left alone, he would never have met the Savior. That he was brought to Christ by his friends or neighbors suggests they cared for him. It was difficult to communicate with, or listen to, the afflicted man. He was deaf, and his speech was extremely difficult to understand.

Such people are not unknown in our generation. John Bunyan, in his book *The Pilgrim's Progress*, described a character whose name was Mr. Talkative. He was a great speaker but it was difficult to listen for the man was shallow and unreliable. He could converse on any subject suitable to the company he kept, and could be devout or blatantly irreligious, as the occasion demanded. The fellow could be equally at home in a bar or a church. It was difficult to correct his behavior, for the man was deaf to all entreaties and blind regarding his need for improvement. Such folk advertise their virtue, and at the same time, remain unacceptable to God. It is difficult to impress them with the importance of the Gospel for they resemble the self-righteous Pharisee.

Mark said Jesus "took him aside from the multitude, and put his fingers into his ears, and he spit, and touched his tongue; and looking up to heaven, he sighed, and saith unto him, . . . Be opened. And straightway his ears were opened, and the string of his tongue was loosed, and he spake plain." It was significant that first the Lord gave hearing. Unless a man can hear the voice of God, his testimony will be useless. Understanding precedes confession in the soul-transforming work of the Almighty. Then the Lord "*charged (commanded) them that they should tell no man*: but the more he charged them, so much the more a great deal they published it; And were beyond measure astonished, saying, He hath done all things well; he maketh both the deaf to hear, and the dumb to speak" (Mark 7:36-37).

Their disobedience might be pardoned, for the excitement of the onlookers was intense. Nevertheless, the Lord had reasons for commanding them to refrain from speaking of what they had witnessed. This event happened between the beginning and the middle of Christ's ministry. Much work had still to be completed, and the Savior was trying to avoid unnecessary problems. Many people desired to make Him their king, but that would have been insurrection against the Romans. The royalist mob would have been overwhelmed by military power, and Palestine would have been a battlefield. The nation could have been divided by civil war, and the purpose of Christ's coming to earth would have been thwarted.

His attitude revealed He was not an agitator seeking to cause strife. His pathway in life led to a Cross, through which He would win an army of redeemed men and women whose endeavors would subjugate the world. Solomon wrote about "a time to keep silence, and a time to speak" (Eccl. 3:7). Evidently the Savior was aware of the truth enunciated by the king of Israel.

The Blind Man at Bethsaida . . . *Condemning* (Mark 8:22-26)

"And he cometh to Bethsaida; and they bring a blind man unto him, and besought him to touch him . . . And he looked up and said, I see men as trees, walking. After that he (Jesus) put his hands again upon his eyes: and he was restored, and saw every man clearly. And Jesus sent him away to his house, saying, *Neither go into the town, nor tell it to any in the town.*"

Bethsaida was one of the nine towns situated at the northern end of the Sea of Galilee. It was a fishing community, but the influx of thousands of people who came to see Jesus brought to them unprecedented prosperity. Thousands of men and women desired to see and hear the new Teacher, and their money was a blessing to the local economy. Probably the citizens became more interested in their increasing profits than in the miracles performed by Jesus. Unlike the Gadarenes who asked the Lord to leave their shores, the people of Bethsaida earnestly desired Him to stay. His presence guaranteed increasing trade. They thought only of larger boats, bigger fishing nets, and luxuries of every form. They would not have appreciated the words of Jesus: "For what is a man profited, if he shall gain the whole world, and lose his own soul? or what shall a man give in exchange for his soul?" (Matt. 16:26).

The people of Bethsaida exploited the situation to increase their wealth, and as the situation deteriorated, the Savior issued one of His sternest warnings. ". . . woe unto thee, Bethsaida! for if the mighty works, which were done in you, had been done in Tyre and Sidon, they would have repented long ago in sackcloth and ashes" (Matt. 11:21). The large crowds brought to the area the greatest business boom in the history of the community, but, unfortunately, love for increasing wealth prevented the people from obtaining treasures more to be desired than gold.

The exact location of Bethsaida has never been discovered, but apparently it was a small village close to Capernaum. Nearby Jesus fed the 5,000 (Luke 9:10-17). It was also the home of Philip (John 12:21). It seems incredible that citizens who had seen so much could be unresponsive to the Lord's message. Jesus commanded the man not to return to Bethsaida, and refrain from witnessing to its people. This was an indictment suggesting that men and women may be very near to the kingdom of God, and yet remain outside.

The Men from the Mountain . . . *How Constrained* (Mark 9:9)

"And as they (the disciples) came down from the mountain, he (Jesus) charged them that *they should tell no man what things they had seen, till the Son of man were risen from the dead.*" The disciples were probably confused when they received this command from their Master. They had witnessed amazing things on the Mount of Transfiguration; had seen and heard Moses and Elijah conversing with the Lord; and had listened to the voice of Jehovah endorsing the character and message of Jesus. They were thrilled and could hardly wait to describe their experience to the disciples who had remained in the valley.

Perhaps the others would not believe. Moses and Elijah had returned to encourage Jesus (Luke 9:30-31). Probably Peter and John were already anticipating the joy of describing the scene in the mount; their next sermons would be sensational!

The Sadducees who did not believe in life beyond the grave would be confounded by the evidence to be supplied. The Savior read their thoughts, and forbade their revealing what had happened during the night. The men stared at their Master, hardly believing what He had said. How could they possibly remain silent when they had so much to tell?

Their emotions were clearly visible when Jesus said: "Do not tell them now, but wait until after I shall have risen from the dead. Then you can tell them everything you know." Why could they not give their testimony prior to His death and resurrection?

(1) *To Protect Unity.* Only three disciples witnessed the transfiguration of Christ; the others remained in the valley overnight. Perhaps they had been entertained by people friendly to Christ, and the opportunity for comfort and food was too good to be refused. If those men heard how Moses and Elias appeared to speak with Jesus, and how the voice of God was heard saying: "This is my beloved Son in Whom I am well pleased; hear ye him," they might have been upset because they had not seen the unique revelation. All kinds of reasons could have been found for blaming Christ and the three disciples who had not called their brethren. Strife could have divided the party, and jealousy would have ruined the fellowship essential to the success of their mission. David was correct when he said: "Behold, how good and how pleasant it is for brethren to dwell together in unity. . . . For there the LORD commanded the blessing" (Ps. 133:1-3).

(2) *To Prevent Arguments.* The Sadducees did not believe in life beyond the grave, and fiercely resisted any doctrine which suggested they were mistaken. The appearance of Moses and Elijah who spoke with the Lord concerning His death, would have contradicted everything taught by the leaders of that sect. Had Peter, James and John commenced explaining what had taken place in the mountain, their opponents would have denied

the account, and accused the preachers of insanity. The whole episode could have created a religious civil war. There would have been arguments at every meeting where the disciples preached, and their influence for Christ and His kingdom would have been destroyed. Few, if any people, would have believed the report, and when nine of the disciples admitted they had no proof of what was being said, Peter, James and John would have appeared to be liars! It was significant that Jesus said they could witness *after the Resurrection*, when the focus of attention would be upon Himself, and not on the ancient saints. The Christians would be able to cite that event as evidence of Christ's death and resurrection, for Moses and Elijah had spoken about the Lord's "decease which he should accomplish at Jerusalem" (Luke 9:30-31).

(3) *To Protect Their Influence.* Jesus knew that after His ascension to heaven, the Holy Spirit would anoint the disciples with power needed for the evangelizing of the world. Evidently, He did not wish their mission to be ruined before it commenced! News spreads quickly and if those men had been accused of lying, preconceived ideas would have warped the minds of the people destined to hear the Gospel. By maintaining silence until after the resurrection of the Lord, the Holy Spirit would be able to prepare them for the stupendous task of world evangelism.

Luke's account of the deliverance of the maniac of Gadara provides a striking contrast to other miracles. "Then the whole multitude of the country of the Gadarenes round about, besought him to depart from them; for they were taken with great fear; and he went up into the ship, and returned back again. Now the man out of whom the devils were departed besought him that he might be with him: but Jesus sent him away saying: *Return to thine own house, and shew how great things God hath done unto thee.* And he went his way, and published throughout the whole city how great things Jesus had done unto him" (Luke 8:37-39, italics mine). The people at Gadara were isolated from the rest of the nation, and it was unlikely their reactions would disturb the rest of the country. The fact that Christ commissioned the man to testify revealed God's mercy is boundless. Although the citizens had requested the Lord to leave their locality, God's love for them remained unchanged.

The disciples were told to refrain from telling their story until the Lord had triumphed over death. That restriction has long since been removed. It was replaced by the Savior's command: "Go ye therefore, and teach all nations, baptizing them in the name of the Father, and of the Son, and of the Holy Ghost. Teaching them to observe all things whatsoever I have commanded you: and, lo, I am with you alway, even unto the end of the world" (Matt. 28:19-20). Professing Christians who never speak about the Lord are disobedient, useless and miserable. They will never hear God saying: "Well done, thou good and faithful servant."

It is significant that some of the most ordinary texts in the Bible are the most suggestive. The Lord was the busiest of all men, but there were occasions when He remained motionless, and each time this happened, something unusual followed. It was often recorded that *"Jesus sat down,"* but five of the references indicated that when He seemed to be doing nothing, He was exceedingly active. The Savior sat down (1) *to weep*; (2) *to welcome*; (3) *to watch*; (4) *to work*; (5) and *to wait*. These verses, studied together, become extremely instructive.

To Weep Over Suffering . . . *How Great His Pain* (Luke 19:35 and 41)

Hundreds of years before the birth of the Savior, the prophet Zechariah wrote: "Rejoice greatly, O daughter of Zion; shout, O daughter of Jerusalem: behold, thy King cometh unto thee; he is just and having salvation; lowly, and riding upon an ass, and upon a colt the foal of an ass" (Zech. 9:9). That remarkable prediction was fulfilled when, on the eve of the Jewish passover, Christ entered Jerusalem. It was truly astonishing that He should ride upon an unbroken colt, and the animal never tried to unseat its Rider.

Possibly, that donkey recognized the Lord of creation, and humbly submitted when Jesus sat upon its back. That display of power was a strange contrast to the tears which later ran down the Lord's face. It was thought-provoking that He should shed tears when confronted by the overthrow of the city. His words were ominous when He said: "If thou hadst known, even thou, at least in this thy day, the things which belong unto thy peace! but now they are hid from thine eyes. For the days shall come upon thee, that thine enemies shall cast a trench about thee, and keep thee in on every side, And shall lay thee even with the ground, and thy children within thee; and they shall not leave in thee one stone upon another; because thou knewest not the time of thy visitation" (Luke 19:42-44). It was sad that even He could do nothing when judgment threatened His people. As He sat upon the donkey, it was evident the approaching tragedy could only have been prevented by the repentance of the nation. Christ remained motionless, because there was nothing He could do to remove the condemnation of the people who rejected Him.

To Welcome a Sinner . . . *How Great His Purpose* (John 4:6)

Jesus had traveled through the oppressive heat of an Eastern midday, and was evidently glad to reach the well at Sychar. John recognized His Master was tired, and when he wrote his Gospel, he reported: "Now Jacob's well was there. Jesus therefore, *being wearied with his journey*, sat thus on the well, and it was about the sixth hour." He had arrived ahead of time and sat patiently awaiting an unpopular woman. He could have proceeded into the city of Sychar, or paused outside. That He sat on the well awaiting the coming of the sinful woman suggested three simple facts. (1) A special visit. (2) A serious vice. (3) A supreme victory.

That notorious sinner became the first female evangelist mentioned in the New Testament. This was evident when, having heard the woman's testimony, the citizens went out to see the Savior, and later exclaimed: ". . . Now we believe, not because of thy saying: for we have heard him ourselves, and know that this is indeed the Christ, the Savior of the world." Other details invite attention.

(1) *How great His foreknowledge.* As far as is known, Christ had never been to that area, and had not met the woman. Nevertheless, He was acquainted with all her circumstances, and knew she was obliged to draw water at the well when other people were absent.

(2) *How gracious His favor.* It was thrilling that, although the neighbors refrained from associating with her, Jesus made special plans to reach that guilty soul. It might have been argued that He could have influenced more people in other places. That may have been true, but since He came into the world to save sinners, it was necessary He would at least attempt to reach individuals whose compelling need was obvious. Had she not come to the well that day, her loss would have been immeasurable.

107

(3) *How glorious His forgiveness.* Jesus did not scold the woman, nor criticize her behavior. Probably, she had been condemned throughout her life; her reputation for lustful associations was widespread. Had the Lord spontaneously criticized her conduct, she would have been unimpressed, and arguments would have closed the entrance to her soul. His pardoning grace overcame her persistent guilt.

Many years have passed since that memorable day in Sychar, but the Savior never changed. It was far more satisfying to speak to one repentant sinner than to address many arrogant Pharisees. He is still seated at His well of salvation hoping other people may follow the woman's example.

To Watch a Sacrifice . . . *How Great His Perception* (Mark 12:41)

Jesus had left the crowded streets of Jerusalem, and had secluded Himself within the temple where He could see without being seen. He was fascinated as He watched people placing their gifts into the temple treasury. The Pharisees, in their flowing robes, were a sight to behold. They never gave anything secretly; they made sure the onlookers knew how much money was being given to God's work. Businessmen, anxious to attract customers, brought gifts, but their faces betrayed the greed in their souls. They gave in obedience to the law, but their money was not gladly offered. They begrudged every shekel placed into the treasury.

The priests, who appealed for increasing generosity, were more interested in finances than in glorifying God. There were occasions when the temple precincts resembled a market, or a financier's office. Then, suddenly, the Lord saw a woman clothed in black garments. Slowly, she approached the treasury and carefully opening her purse, produced two small and insignificant coins. She was an impoverished widow. The Lord knew that when she offered two mites, she had nothing left.

When Mark recalled the incident, he wrote: "And Jesus sat over against the treasury: and beheld how people cast money into the treasury: and many that were rich cast in much. And there came a certain poor widow, and she threw in two mites,

108

which make a farthing. And he called unto him his disciples, and saith unto them, Verily, I say unto you, That this poor widow hath cast more in, than all they which have cast into the treasury. For all they did cast in of their abundance; but she of her want, did cast in all that she had, even all her living" (Mark 12:41-44). His assessment of her contribution was astonishing, and yet, His reasoning was easy to understand. Even Samuel had heard God saying: ". . . the Lord seeth not as man seeth; for man looketh on the outward appearance, but the Lord looketh on the heart" (1 Sam. 16:7). The widow's gift was sanctified and multiplied by her love. Christ still assesses the gifts of His people. Since He gave His all for us, we should never offer anything less than the best to Him.

To Work for the Sick . . . *How Great His Power* (Matt. 15:29)

The Lord had returned from His memorable visit to Tyre and Sidon, and, reaching Capernaum, had climbed into the mountains overlooking the Sea of Galilee. Someone recognized Him, and soon the news of His arrival spread throughout the nearby cities. Within a short time, crowds followed Him into the hill, taking with them sick relatives and friends. It was remarkable that Jesus was able to heal many people, and the diversity of patients suggested many possibilities.

There were lame people who were limited in their movements. Something had interfered with their capabilities; it was difficult to do what once they did easily. Within the Christian church these might be identified as backsliders! Others had never seen; they lived in the dark, listening to information related by other folk. They resembled unconverted people who had never seen the Savior. They heard His message but had no knowledge of His ability to open blind eyes.

Some who could see and walk had difficulty speaking; they were dumb, like secret disciples! Matthew mentioned the maimed—people who had been hurt by the unkind circumstances of life. The term was indefinite, and probably covered many kinds of injuries. Yet, no task was too hard for the Savior; His ability was without limitation.

Furthermore, there is no record that any of the people healed ever became sick again. Frequently Christ commanded people to "*go and sin no more*," but in every instance there was nothing misleading about His miracles. Unfortunately, modern faith-healers can attend the funerals of people supposedly healed a few weeks before their decease. Matthew was wise when he spoke of the "*many others*" healed by the Savior.

To Wait for Supremacy . . . *How Great His Patience* (Heb. 12:10)

The Savior had reached Journey's End! Calvary and the resurrection were memories. He had ascended into heaven; been welcomed by innumerable angels; crowned with glory and honor, and installed as the High Priest of His people. Serenity was upon His face; expectancy shone in His eyes; God had promised that even His enemies would become His footstool. Christ would become the King of Kings and Lord of Lords, and He was destined to inherit the kingdoms of the entire world. Confidently, and patiently, He sat on the right hand of the Majesty on High.

Yet, it was significant that He *stood* to welcome home the first martyr. Describing the death of Stephen, Luke wrote: "But he (Stephen), being full of the Holy Ghost, looked up steadfastly into heaven, and saw the glory of God, and Jesus *standing* on the right hand of God. And said, Behold, I see the heavens opened, and the Son of Man *standing* on the right hand of God" (Acts 7:55-56). Evidently, God desired to draw attention to the fact that although the High-Priestly ministry of the Savior was important, it could not deprive Christ of the privilege of welcoming to heaven the brave Christian who laid down his life for the Master.

When Paul was nearing the end of his life, he wrote remarkable words to Timothy. "For I am now ready to be offered, and the time of my departure is at hand. I have fought a good fight, I have finished my course, I have kept the faith: Henceforth there is laid up for me a crown of righteousness, which the Lord, the righteous judge, shall give me at that day: and not to me only, but unto all them also that love his appearing" (2 Tim.

4:6-8). It would be interesting if we could know the kind of reception which awaits us when we also reach our Homeland.

Dr. Egerton Young, who ministered to Indian tribes, told an interesting story of what happened one day when he had, apparently, failed to influence the people. He said: "I visited a band of Indians in the far north, and found them to be utterly unresponsive to the Gospel, until I shouted: 'I know where all your children are — your dead children.' Quickly, they manifested intense interest. I continued: 'They have gone from your wigwams and your campfires. Your hearts are sad, and you mourn for the children you hear not. But there is only one way to the beautiful land, where the Son of God has gone, and into which He takes the children, and you must come this way, if you would be happy and enter in.' As I spoke, a stalwart Indian sprang up and rushed toward me. He said: 'Missionary, my heart is empty, and I mourn much, for none of my children are left among the living. I am very lonely in my wigwam; I long to see them again, and hold them in my arms. Tell me, what must I do to enter that beautiful land, and see my children?' Others quickly followed him, seeking instruction" (quoted from *One Hundred Great Texts and Their Treatment*, pg. 279). There was placed on Dean Alford's tombstone a beautiful inscription. *"The inn of a traveler on his way to Jerusalem."*

Jesus met all types of people, and His remarks concerning them were always interesting. A kingdom is a territory over which someone is sovereign. Within the Bible, the term may relate to an established domain on earth; to the Church over which Christ reigns as Lord, or even to the sanctuary of the human soul. The Hebrews believed it related exclusively to the Jewish race, and were displeased with the teaching that God could reside within human hearts (Luke 17:21).

The term *kingdom* is better defined by *a presence than a place*. Some people accepted the Lord's teaching and hurried into God's kingdom. Others rejected it because they disliked the new interpretation, and many remained undecided whether to advance or retreat. Some people reached the entrance to God's kingdom, but failed to enter. The text suggests: (1) A Desired Destiny; (2) A Disturbing Doubt and (3) A Disastrous Delay.

The Concerned Man . . . *who was very near*
(Mark 12:28-34)

"And when Jesus saw that he (the scribe) answered discreetly, he said unto him, Thou art not far from the kingdom of God . . ." (Mark 12:28-34). Scribes were among the most important people in Israel. They wrote or copied the scriptures, and were often required to interpret their writings. Occasionally, and under special circumstances, they became judges, for their legal knowledge enabled them to decide cases in the courts. Evidently, one of these men overheard remarks when the Sadducees endeavored to trick Jesus into making rash statements. The scribe, who might have been a Pharisee, perceived the Lord was fair in His replies to the arrogant interrogators, and proceeded to ask another question: "Which is the first commandment of all?" He agreed with the Savior's answer, and his response impressed the Lord. The scribe was not a bigoted zealot; he was a seeker after truth, and he was not afraid to express appreciation of the Savior. He exclaimed, "Well, Master, thou hast said the truth; for there is one God; and there is none other but he." Jesus recognized the man's sincerity, and said: "Thou art not far from the kingdom of God." It would be interesting to know whether or not the scribe ever entered into the kingdom. He could have been within inches only to miss it by a mile!

The Challenged Man . . . *who was almost in!* (Mark 10:17-23)

"And a certain ruler asked him, saying, Good Master, what shall I do to inherit eternal life?" His conversation with the Lord revealed that even Christ admired the integrity of the man who said he had always obeyed the commandments of God. "Then Jesus beholding him, loved him." The ruler was morally commendable, but his initial statement was not as accurate as it seemed to be. He claimed he had loved his God with all his heart, soul and mind, but when he was asked to forsake his wealth and become an itinerant preacher, his love of money superseded his affection for Jehovah. He was certainly close to the kingdom of God—but not close enough!

Some years ago, an edition of *The Presbyterian Banner* carried an exciting story of an astonishing discovery made near the ruins of Pompeii, Italy. It was reported that workmen digging a foundation for a new building outside the area of the buried city, found the petrified body of a woman whose hands were full of jewels. Evidently, the anxious lady had tried to save her jewels, but was caught and buried in the downpour of hot ashes. The jewels were excellently preserved, having been protected by the body. The workmen found bracelets, necklaces, rings, amulets studded with gems, and a pair of earrings which were unique. Each earring contained twenty-one perfect pearls, set in gold, in imitation of a bunch of grapes. It was tragic to see a petrified corpse still grasping the jewels. Evidently the anxious woman had returned to save her gems, but, in so doing, lost her life.

The Cautious Man . . . *who stopped just outside!* (Acts 5:34-40)

The council-chamber was in an uproar; men were standing

and shouting; the chairman was helpless when he endeavored to restore order to the assembly. Two upstart heretics had ignored the authority of the council, and their defiance had incensed the leaders of the nation. Peter and his colleagues stood in the midst of the screaming councilors, and their attitude indicated they had no intention to obey anybody except Christ.

"Then stood there up one in the council, a Pharisee, named Gamaliel, a doctor of the law, had in reputation among all the people, and commanded to put the apostles forth a little space" (Acts 5:34). It seemed miraculous when the noise subsided and the frustrated, angry representatives became silent. All eyes were focused on the eminent Doctor, who was probably the most respected member in the assembly. His quiet, insistent advice was as effective as a king commanding his subjects. "Yes, Gamaliel would know what to do with these despicable rebels!"

His short speech was tremendous; his tones authoritative; his logic unanswerable. He said: "Ye men of Israel, take heed to yourselves what ye intend to do as touching these men." With convincing words he calmed their ruffled spirits, and his concluding remarks were inspiring. "Refrain from these men, and let them alone; for if this counsel or this work be of men, it will come to nought: But if it be of God, ye cannot overthrow it; lest haply ye be found even to fight against God. And to him they agreed: and when they had called the apostles, and beaten them, they commanded that they should not speak in the name of Jesus, and let them go" (Acts 5:38-40). Gamaliel saved the apostles' lives, but his policy of procrastination could not be commended. How long should his hearers wait before deciding whether or not the preachers were men of God? How much evidence was needed to overthrow the preconception of critics who never intended to change their opinions?

Gamaliel was the greatest theologian in Israel, but one of his students was named Saul. He had come from Tarsus to study under the influence of the famous teacher. This young man became a fierce persecutor, and his attacks on the Christians were known by every citizen in the country. Whether or not Gamaliel approved of such ferocity is extremely doubtful, but he had no authority to condemn what the high priest had sanctioned. When Saul was miraculously transformed, the president of the Hebrew seminary knew his best student had become an advocate of the new faith. Probably he who had been so close to the Kingdom of God, stopped in its entrance, when fear paralyzed his feet!

When the governor of one of our great states unexpectedly visited a Sunday school convention, the audience applauded his entry, and requested a speech. The man had no prepared manuscript, but he stood on the platform and said: "Friends, I really have nothing to say, but I am heartily in sympathy with your work, and I can at least stand up and be counted." Gamaliel, an inferior man, was handicapped. He could neither stand nor advance.

The Condemned Man . . . *who had no desire to enter!*
(Luke 23:32)

It has often been claimed that whereas the sun softens wax, it hardens clay. Paul said of Christ and the gospel: "For we are unto God a sweet savour of Christ, in them that are saved, and in them that perish: To the one we are the savour of death unto death; and to the other the savour of life unto life" (2 Cor. 2:15-16).

The glorious gospel of God's grace either redeems or repels, and in support of that fact, it is only necessary to consider Christ's companions in death. Two criminals were close to the Savior of the world. One was near enough to hear Christ's voice and respond to His love, the other was far away and unreachable. The conversion of the one man revealed a magnificent triumph of God's grace; the other, whose cursing was only silenced by death, expressed a tragedy of unresponsiveness. One man, accompanied by his greatest Friend, went into the kingdom of God; the other, into the gloom of a hopeless eternity. Yet, that unrepentant sinner was within two or three yards of the entrance to God's kingdom. The overflowing heart of the Redeemer was only a prayer away. C. D. Martin truly expressed the situation when he wrote:

So near to the kingdom of heaven,
Yet halting at the door.
Oh, shall your soul through doubting
Be lost for ever more?

The Convicted Man . . . *who was afraid to enter!*
(Acts 26:28)

For a little while Paul was very excited, for it appeared he was about to win a sensational convert. He had been permitted to testify before a glamorous audience. Agrippa had come to stay with Festus, the Roman governor, and a special interview had been arranged in which Paul would be permitted to speak. His entire future could easily rest upon the results of his preaching that day.

The listener became convicted by the Spirit of God, and, exultantly, Paul cried: "King Agrippa, believest thou the prophets? I know that thou believest." The monarch was restless; his eyes were staring at the questioner, and every person present knew Paul had not preached in vain. Agrippa frowned. Why had he gotten himself into such a situation? The challenging eyes of the prisoner seemed to be piercing his soul; he could not remain mute. "Then Agrippa said unto Paul, Almost thou persuadest me to be a Christian."

His testimony that Paul might have been released had he not appealed to Caesar, was an excuse. How could he embrace the doctrines of Paul when they violated every Roman law? How could he accept the prisoner's Savior and permit the preacher to remain shackled? Unwise and premature action could be harbingers of disaster; people throughout the nation would spread the news of the king's leniency, and that could lead to undesired repercussions. The troubled man thought only of his own welfare, and he forgot his eternal destiny. He was close enough to the kingdom of God to see within its portals, but he remained a troubled coward.

Many years ago, the British sailing ship, *Royal Charter*, after a voyage around the world, was approaching its home port of Liverpool. At that time, Dr. William M. Taylor was a pastor in that city, and the wife of the first mate was a member of his church. Crowds of people waited throughout the night to welcome the men who had navigated the vessel through many hazards. Alas, the ship sank during the night, and a devastated nation mourned its loss. When news of the tragedy was confirmed, Dr. Taylor was asked to break the news to the family of the first mate. As he laid his finger upon the bell, the door was suddenly opened by a small girl who excitedly exclaimed: "Oh, Dr. Taylor, I thought it was my papa; he is coming home today." The preacher felt he was like an executioner entering the home. The table was set for breakfast, and the lady of the house stepped forward to say: "Dr. Taylor, this is indeed a privilege. If you will wait a little while, perhaps you will sit at our table with us. My husband was on the *Royal Charter*, and he will be home soon."

Dr. Taylor looked at her for a moment, and then said: "Poor woman, your husband will never come home. The *Royal Charter* went down last night, and your husband sank with the ship." The lady grasped her head; staggered for a moment, and as she slumped to the floor, said: "*Oh my God, so near home and then lost*" (condensed from *One Hundred Texts and Their Treatment*, J. Wilbur Chapman, pg. 232).

THOU SHALT CALL HIS NAME ... Jesus (LUKE 1:31)

Many years ago, I heard a missionary describing what happened after she had spent a day among people who had never heard of Jesus. She had returned to the mission and lay awake thinking of the Indian women to whom she had spoken at the village well. Suddenly, she heard someone approaching the house, and, going out to investigate, met a man who asked: "Teacher, what was His name?" He said: "You told our women about a great Man Who healed the sick and was kind to everybody. What was His name?"

The young lady responded: "Jesus."

"Ah," he said: "That's it, that's it. Jesus. Jesus. Jesus," and repeating that name over and over again, the dusky visitor began the seven mile journey back to his village.

> Jesus is the sweetest name I know:
> And He's just the same, as His lovely name.
> And that's the reason why I love Him so,
> For Jesus is the sweetest name I know.

Through His Name ... *Instant Pardon* (1 John 2:12)

John was an old man who loved to remember! He had seen and heard the Word; he had watched the growth of the church; and he had survived many storms. He smiled; his children were waiting to hear news of their spiritual father. What could he write to them? Suddenly, his face reflected the glory in his soul. He would tell them more about the Master and write about *the precious Name*. "I write unto you little children, because *your sins are forgiven you for his name's sake*" (1 John 2:12). In a moment they had received what a lifetime of effort failed to provide. John emphasized their sins *had been* forgiven — they were gone! Throughout their early life, those converts strenuously endeavored to obey the law, but the rigid requirements of Moses only condemned them. The observance of ritualistic procedure, the offering of turtledoves and lambs, only intensified the yearnings of their souls. They had struggled to reach the unreachable, and they cherished an impossible dream. Then they met Jesus, Who provided a gift which riches

118

could never purchase. "Yes," said John, "I will tell them about the Lord."

The testimony of a Chicago derelict should never be forgotten. His drinking and debauchery had driven him from his family and home. Then one night he stumbled into the Pacific Garden Mission in Chicago and heard someone singing: "There's a wideness in God's mercy." When the meeting was over, he went to the home where his wife lived with her father. He lay in the backyard all night hoping to catch a glimpse of his children. He said later: "As the eastern sky began to blush, the old song kept ringing in my ears. Then, instead of creeping up to the window, I just crept up to the feet of Jesus, and He didn't scold me; He knew I had been scolded enough. He didn't pity me, and He didn't give me any advice. He knew I'd had plenty of that. He just put His arms around my neck and loved me. And when the sun arose I was a new man."

Through His Name . . . *Inspired Prayer* (John 14:13-14)

John was reminiscing again; his eyes were pools of thought! He was listening once more to Jesus. "Hitherto ye have asked nothing in my name." It was true that often he had gone to the temple to pray, but his petitions had only been passing thoughts. God remained inscrutable and distant. Then came the day when John met the Savior, Who said: "And whatsoever ye shall ask in my name, that will I do, that the Father may be glorified in the Son. If ye shall ask anything in my name, I will do it" (John 14:13-14). The name of Jesus evidently commanded attention in heaven. It was the key which supplied admittance to every room in the heavenly palace, the operator who put through every call to the Father; the endorsement upon every check which guaranteed to supply the needs of Christians. The patriarchs had prayed, and often in a miraculous fashion, their prayers were answered.

The teaching of Jesus revealed new and wonderful truths about the privileges of intercession. It was simple, sure, sacred. Men could pray at any time, anywhere; the Father was not in a remote part of the heavens; He was close to every follower of the Savior. The Name of Christ guaranteed a welcome in the

119

very Holy of Holies, and introduced an experience hitherto unknown.

Some years ago, a ship was wrecked off the coast of Essex, in England. A thick fog obliterated the coast line, and, as a last resort, the captain ordered his men to tie themselves to the rigging of the vessel. Finally he said: "I have done everything to save you." A boy replied, "Skipper, you have not prayed!" The captain then offered a simple, but desperate prayer for deliverance. He looked at his watch and the time was 1:25 A.M. Unknown to the crew, at that precise moment a coastguardsman peering through the fog saw the ship, and reported the matter to the authorities. A lifeboat went to rescue the sailors, and the captain, publicly thanking God, mentioned the time when he prayed for help. The coastguardsman overheard the captain's statement and knew God had miraculously answered prayer. Even weather conditions can be changed by the mighty Name of Jesus. (Reprinted from the author's book, *Bible Windows*, pages 83-84, Kregel Publications.)

Through His Name . . . *Increasing Power* (Acts 3:16)

John was smiling; he was with his brother Simon Peter walking to the temple. They saw a beggar sitting by the wayside. The poor man lived on the fringe of things; he knew about the sanctuary, but was content to live outside! He knew the priests, but never availed himself of their services. Perhaps he gave donations for the upkeep of the sanctuary, but his real interest was making money! He was a businessman who appreciated the temple because it brought him into contact with gullible people. Perhaps he was an untrained psychologist, and knew that people going to worship would be likely to help his cause; it made them feel good! Had the beggar lived in modern times, he might have raised millions of dollars. When he saw two men approaching, his eyes shone. When John remembered the incident, he smiled. His brother Simon Peter had been equal to the occasion.

"And Peter, fastening his eyes upon him with John, said, Look on us. And he gave heed unto them, expecting to receive something of them. Then Peter said, Silver and gold have I none; but such as I have give I thee: In the name of Jesus Christ of Nazareth rise up and walk. And he took him by the right hand, and lifted him up; and immediately his feet and ankle bones received strength. And he leaping up stood, and entered with them into the temple, walking, and leaping, and praising God" (Acts 3:4-8). The memory of that remarkable miracle could never fade. Power through the name of Jesus had accomplished the impossible. The beggar, who had been lame from birth, found new agility and desire. He discovered a new type of wealth as he drew nearer to the altar of God.

I shall never forget the businessman in South Africa who entertained his friends at a special bar installed in his home. He was a church member who lived a beggar's life on the outside of reality. After his conversion, he removed the liquor and transformed his bar into a pulpit! Life in a gutter is never attractive!

Through His name . . . *Indomitable Passion* (3 John 7)

John's mood had changed; his smiles had given place to indignation. Conditions within the churches had altered. Small men with enlarged egos were usurping authority, and the cause of Christ was in jeopardy. Brave young men had become evangelists, but, unfortunately, a man named Diotrephes had been a stumbling block to the crusaders. John disliked this attitude and said: "I wrote unto the church: but Diotrephes, who loveth to have the preeminence among them, received us not." The apostle's face was sad; it was a disgrace that any man should refuse to help Christ's ambassadors, who, *"for his name's sake . . .* went forth, taking nothing of the Gentiles." These evangelists were risking their lives every day; the possibility of their becoming martyrs was real. Others were destined to be fed to ravenous beasts, or burnt at stakes in the emperor's gardens. That was to be expected, but to face beasts of another kind within the churches was unacceptable.

Dictators had become important, and any who opposed them were removed. Other preachers might have turned back, but these intrepid evangelists were unafraid. They loved Christ, and "for His name's sake" went forth depending upon the promises of the Lord. The fire within their hearts could not be extinguished.

During the ministry of the China Inland Mission, a doctor from a missionary hospital told a remarkable story. One of his patients had cataracts removed from his eyes. Gratefully, the man returned to his home. A few months later, 48 blind men, each clinging to a rope, were led into the hospital compound by the former patient. They had walked 250 miles to meet the great doctor. Energized by an increasing compassion, the first patient had "evangelized" his area to tell to blind people the glorious news. He not only informed his friends; he led them, at great cost, to the source of his blessing. The wonderful Name of Jesus has always supplied the inspiration which made such acts possible.

A REED SHAKEN BY THE WIND   (LUKE 7:19-24).

This story concerning John the Baptist is one of the most dramatic in the Bible. Although the following names may be meaningless to most people, the fact that Ambrose, Hilary, Chrysostom, Theophylact, Calvin, Beza and Melancthon discussed the incident and wrote their findings for posterity, proves that John's request fascinated the religious scholars of successive generations. More recently the debates continued with Meyer, Ewald, Godet, Plumptre, Farrar and others, and apparently, so to speak, John the Baptist started a ball rolling which never stopped. To say the least, his question to Jesus: "Art thou he that should come?" created unprecedented problems.

John had been imprisoned for approximately 18 months and lived alone with his memories. Beneath the blue skies of Galilee he had preached to enormous crowds, and for a while at least, had been the central figure in Israel. His forthright presentation of truth, his unshakable faith and courage, won an abiding place in the hearts of all listeners. Soldiers, priests and statesmen attended his services, and John's exploits were discussed in every Hebrew home. His dynamic ministry stirred every part of the nation; he had been God's anointed ambassador. Unfortunately, that time of spiritual refreshing had been replaced by solitude and incarceration in Herod's dungeon. Everything had changed dramatically, and for prolonged periods of time, John's only companions were the spiders who spun their webs in the corners of his cell. When the prisoner reminisced and relived the experiences he had known in the Jordan Valley, his mind — so some theologians believe — became a prey to doubt.

Occasionally John's disciples were permitted to visit their master, but their conversation never promoted comfort and confidence. They were his only means of communicating with the outside world, but alas, they brought disconcerting news of current events. "Master," said one of his friends, "do you remember that Carpenter from Nazareth whom you baptized? You suggested He would be our Messiah. Did you make a mistake? It would be extremely difficult to find a more unlikely

123

candidate for that position. That man neither speaks nor acts like a king of Israel. You denounced hypocrites; He dines with them. We expected Him to expel our enemies, but He fraternizes with them. John, is it possible that you were mistaken when you led us to believe He would deliver Israel?"

"And John calling unto him two of his disciples, sent them to Jesus saying: Art thou he that should come or look we for another?" Throughout the history of the church, theologians have inquired: "Did John ask that question because his faith had weakened, or did he send his friends knowing the Lord alone could solve their problems?" Later, when Christ replied to the question, He said: "What went ye out into the wilderness for to see — a reed shaken by the wind?" The banks of the Jordan River were lined with plants of many kinds, and when the winds blew through the valley, the rustle of the reeds could easily be heard. They swayed and leaned with the breeze. Had John been a shaking, bending reed? Some teachers believe his faith, temporarily, had weakened.

The Wind of Adversity . . . *The danger of doubt*

During World War II, Wales was extensively damaged by German bombs. Beautiful homes were reduced to rubble, and the town of Swansea was obliterated. It was annoying to hear people grumbling and asking: "Why did God permit this to happen?" Many of the questioners never attended any church and scoffed at religion. Yet, in times of trouble, they blamed God Whom they had ignored.

There is a great difference between a shaking reed and an unyielding oak tree, yet there are people who resemble both. Birds may nest safely in a tree, but a shaking reed is a poor haven in a tempest. Did John become increasingly despondent as he listened to the depressing conversation of his friends? Did he permit their biased opinions to darken the blue sky of his serenity? When his faith weakened, did he dispatch his friends on a regrettable errand?

When I was a young Christian, the son of our pastor came to stay in our home. His parents were away on business, and my mother consented to care for the small boy during their absence. When it was time for the lad to go to bed, I listened and smiled when he prayed: "Oh, God, I'm not going to pray to *You* anymore. You do not answer my prayers anyhow. I asked *You* last night that I should have all my sums right today, and I had two wrong. It's no good asking *You* anything!" That small child was a forerunner of many older people with similar complaints. On the other hand, there is in the forest a vine which wraps itself around oak trees. It matters not from which direction the wind blows, the vine is either sheltered by the tree or pressed closer to it. It is better to cling than complain!

The Wind of Hypocrisy . . . *The disaster of defiance*

One day, when I was visiting homes in a rural area of Herefordshire, I met a very hospitable Irishman who expressed interest in the Gospel. He was so enthusiastic that I asked why he had not attended my meetings in the nearby Methodist church. Instantly, his countenance changed as he replied, "Oh no, I will never enter that place again. I have not been inside those doors for *fifteen* years." I asked what had happened at that time, and he cited an argument with a church leader. With God's help I brought those stubborn men together and that evening saw four people surrendering to Christ. The incident reminded me of what happened when the sons of Israel's high priest disgraced their calling.

". . . the sin of the young men was very great before the LORD; for men abhorred the offering of the LORD" (1 Sam. 2:17). At that early period in Jewish history there were no synagogues throughout the nation, and if men desired to visit the house of God, they journeyed to Shiloh to attend one of the festivals. People anticipated the occasion, for it became a religious vacation when they met friends from all over the country. When the evil conduct of the priests became known, citizens detested the improprieties, and many families refused to obey the commandment to be present at Shiloh. The shekinah glory might be residing over the Tabernacle, but the winds of hypocrisy had blown it from the hearts of men and women. They saw the offenders but lost sight of the Lord.

The Wind of Complicity . . . *The defeat in departing*

"For Demas hath forsaken me, having loved this present world, and is departed unto Thessalonica" (2 Tim. 4:10). Poor Demas, a yearning heart had destroyed his happiness. The drudgery of serving a prisoner irritated his soul, and in his restlessness, he found the beckoning night-lights of the world too glamorous to resist.

Perhaps he believed the approaching death of Paul would leave him without sustenance. What could be done if he were left alone in an alien city? Maybe Demas longed to participate in pleasures which Paul condemned. The women, wine and songs of Rome were attractive, but how could he enjoy the attractions of the city when his friend remained in a prison cell?

Then he thought of an alternative. He would go to Thessalonica, and be free to do whatever he desired. It may never be known how he felt when he made his final visit to the apostle. His eyes were furtive; his face flushed as he tried to conceal the uneasiness within his soul.

He had become a reed shaken by the wind, and although he did not yet realize the magnitude of his mistake, he was destined to regret his action. He deserted his best friend, and denied the Lord. Throughout the history of the church millions of professing Christians, unfortunately, have emulated his example.

If the pleasures of the world can be likened to a tree, then its fruits are numerous. An excessive desire to make money either by legitimate or illegitimate means; a desire to reach the top of a profession at any cost; the surrendering of spiritual convictions to enjoy something prohibited by the Word of God; or an illicit association which saps moral and spiritual strength. These are the adverse winds which prove whether a man is a shaking reed or a dependable Christian.

Mr. Robert Robinson, who wrote the hymn, "Come, Thou fount of every blessing," unfortunately became a reed shaken by the wind. He lost his communion with God, and in an attempt to alleviate his misery, traveled around the world. He met a young lady who asked what he thought of her favorite hymn, and was astonished to discover she had fallen in love with his own composition. He tried to evade her question, but she insisted on obtaining an answer. Finally, he confessed he was the author of those verses, but he had lost the joy of serving Christ. The young Christian reminded the sorrowful man that *"the streams of mercy"* mentioned in his hymn were still flowing. That girl changed his life, and the shaken reed found new stability in Christ.

Some theologians believe John had been influenced by the winds of adversity, but the evidence supporting that conclusion is not irrefutable. Dr. G. Campbell Morgan and many other illustrious teachers rejected that idea, affirming that John never wavered from his initial convictions and was undisturbed by the events which resulted in his imprisonment and death.

John knew what would happen even before he was arrested by Herod. He announced: "He must increase, but I must decrease" (John 3:30). God revealed to His servant the identity of the Messiah, and evidently imparted knowledge concerning the nature of His sacrificial ministry. John announced to his listeners that the Carpenter was "The Lamb of God which would take away the sins of the world" (John 1:29) and the idea that the evangelist lost his faith is unacceptable.

John's Witness . . . *the tremendous message*

When an angel predicted the birth of John the Baptist, he said: ". . . he shall be filled with the Holy Ghost, *even from his mother's womb"* (see Luke 1:15). It is beyond comprehension that, even in embryonic form, John was controlled by the Spirit of God. That child grew to be the official representative of the Almighty, and wherever and whenever he ministered, the Lord endorsed what he did and said. He possessed a spiritual insight that few men had. His statement, "Behold the Lamb of God that taketh away the sins of the world," indicated the sacrifices in former dispensations pointed to Christ; that, whereas they met the need of individuals, Jesus became the Savior of the world. The wilderness preacher was controlled by the Almighty, but he knew his own ministry would soon terminate. His statement, "He must increase, I must decrease," said all that needed to be said. It is unlikely that such a man would be influenced by the gossip of a few disappointed disciples.

John's Worry . . . *the troubled men*

It was always unwise to argue with people already convinced! The followers of John were not only disappointed by the demise of their leader; they were jealous of the Man Who succeeded him. Their enthusiasm had been limitless, and it was difficult to understand why their leader should be imprisoned while Another inherited his popularity. Perhaps those troubled men felt they had been robbed of pre-eminence in a national revival. The disciples of John missed the thrills of attending their master's meetings; life had become empty and meaningless.

John welcomed his visitors, but frowned when he realized the cause of their despondency. What could be done to help them? He would send them to Jesus, Who would know how to dispel their doubts. "Brothers," he said, "will you do something for me? Go and ask Jesus if He is the Messiah, and tell Him I sent you." John smiled and said to himself: "The Lord will know what to do." "And in that same hour he (Jesus) cured many of their infirmities and plagues, and of evil spirits; and unto many that were blind he gave sight. Then Jesus answering said unto them, Go your way, and tell John what things ye have seen and heard; how that the blind see, the lame walk, the lepers are cleansed, the deaf hear, the dead are raised, to the poor the gospel is preached. *And blessed is he, whosoever shall not be offended in me*" (Luke 7:21-23, italics mine).

John's Wisdom . . . *the thrilling Master*

"And when the messengers of John were departed, he (Jesus) began to speak unto the people concerning John, What went ye out into the wilderness for to see? A reed shaken with the wind? . . . I say unto you, Among those that are born of women there is not a greater prophet than John the Baptist: but he that is least in the kingdom of God is greater than he" (Luke 7:24, 28). That strange, yet wonderful utterance, caused endless discussion among theologians. It is difficult to believe the most insignificant, uneducated believer in an African village would be greater than the man who foreran the Savior! Others believe Jesus referred to Himself; that since He assumed the lowest place among men, He was still much greater than John.

There is no problem in the words of the Lord. Christ came to establish a new spiritual order: the kingdom of God on earth. He created something hitherto unknown: a realm to which John never belonged. Jesus emphasized that, *where* a man was exceeded the importance of *what* he was! The least *inside* the kingdom was greater than the greatest *outside* the kingdom. John was not a reed shaken by the wind; leaning one way today, and another tomorrow. Christ's commendation was not a cover-up! John stood tall in the sight of God, but the question may be asked — How tall is tall?

An edition of *The Sunday School Times* carried an interesting story. Centuries ago two boys named Martin came into contact with Christ. One of them, later known as Martin of Basle, wrote on a piece of parchment: "O most merciful Christ. I know I can be saved only by the merit of Thy precious blood. Holy Jesus, I acknowledge Thy sufferings for me. I love Thee; I love Thee." He removed a stone from a wall in his house, and hid his message. It was discovered 100 years later when the home was demolished.

The other boy was Martin Luther, who said: "My Lord has confessed me before men. I will not shrink from confessing Him before kings." Today, everybody reveres the memory of Luther, but *Martin of Basle* remains only a name. It would not be difficult to decide which of the two men resembled the evangelist who cried: "Behold the Lamb of God which taketh away the sin of the world."

Someone has said that "Conscience is the whisper of God in the soul of man," and if that statement be true, it is the world's greatest preacher. Webster's Dictionary defines conscience as "the faculty, power or principle which decides on the lawfulness or unlawfulness of actions, with a compulsion to do right. It is the moral judgment which prohibits or opposes the violation of a previously recognized ethical principle." Millions of people know that conscience is the watchdog which refuses to remain silent in the presence of an intruder; the divinely installed equipment within the human brain which emits warnings when man is tempted; the siren which awakens a sleeper when the sanctity of his soul is being threatened. It is controlled by an unseen operator, who, whether we like it not, sounds an alarm which foolish people ignore.

The Pharisees ... *Who Realized Their Predicament* (John 8:6-9)

"But Jesus stooped down, and with his finger wrote on the ground, as though he heard them not. So when they continued asking him, he lifted up himself, and said unto them, He that is without sin among you, let him first cast a stone at her. And they which heard it, being convicted by their own conscience, went out one by one, beginning at the eldest, even unto the last: and Jesus was left alone, and the woman standing in the midst."

The Pharisees were very smug, conceited and confident as they looked at Jesus. Their eyes reflected the hardness of their hearts; they were cynical. A woman of ill-fame had been pushed into the presence of the Lord, and her accusers were merciless when they said: "Master, this woman was taken in adultery, in the very act. Now Moses in the law commanded us that such should be stoned: but what sayest thou?" Their strategy had been carefully planned — possibly by one of their legal advisers; it could not be defeated. If the Savior said: "Stone her," they would have done so immediately knowing His command would contradict His teaching. If He refused to obey the law, they could arrest Him for contempt of the legal system., Apparently their scheme was foolproof. They were cynical, haughty, hypocritical and callous. They could not have known the Divine Operator was about to ruin their carefully laid plan.

Maybe even the disciples smiled for the scene was strange. The Master's reply had shattered the pride of the accusers. Even the most important among them was suddenly disconcerted for that kneeling preacher had discovered their closely guarded secrets. He knew about things which, if made public, could create scandal. Fearing that at any moment Jesus might begin accusing individuals, the Pharisees commenced leaving the area. The eldest went first — they had lived longer than the others — and had more to hide! Had they thrown stones at the woman, the Teacher might have condemned them publicly, and that would have been disastrous. They frowned; their consciences were becoming troublesome.

Simon Peter . . . *Who Reached the Porch* (Mark 14:67-68)

If one might be permitted to mix metaphors, it can be said that Peter was skating on thin ice, and was about to fall into hot water! Proud, indignant and very confident, the apostle had vehemently said he would never disown his Master. The idea that such a deed was possible was preposterous. He had never failed anyone, and would not begin with the Lord. Now he had wandered into enemy territory, and was fraternizing with enemies. He was a fish out of water!

The attack upon his integrity was sudden and devastating. Peter was dumbfounded. Memories flooded his mind, and anguish brought tears to his eyes. Then a voice began to whisper within his soul, and the agitated man failed to silence the accusations. Suddenly, he began to move toward the door, and within a few moments reached the porch where the breezes of the night began to cool his brow. The stars were shining in the darkened sky, and Peter trembled as he remembered his denial at the fire. There is reason to believe that his conscience urged the troubled man to remain outside, but when he reentered the hall, his way of escape closed.

Why did he take that short but vital walk toward the porch? It could not have been a premeditated act. The lights of warning were beginning to glow within his soul; the grace of God was endeavoring to prevent a tragedy. The apostle never forgot that terrible occasion; he felt guilty for the rest of his life. The Lord always provides a way of escape for His people, but when men and women refuse to avail themselves of that kindness, increasing sorrow becomes inevitable.

Herod . . . *Who Remembered the Past* (Matthew 14:1-2)

"At that time Herod the tetrarch heard of the fame of Jesus, And said unto his servants, This is John the Baptist; he is risen from the dead; and therefore mighty works do shew forth themselves in him."

The king was frightened; his mind was in a turmoil; his confidence was shattered, and his future threatened. The murder of John the Baptist had left an indelible stain on the monarch's conscience, and Herod could not forget the birthday party when he had gazed upon the decapitated head of the prophet. He was afraid to close his eyes at night for he believed retribution to be inevitable. The slain preacher had risen from the dead to avenge what had been done in the palace. The monarch had made inquiries concerning Jesus of Nazareth, but what he had ascertained confirmed his greatest fear. A ghost was about to take his life; he was doomed! Herod thought of the unpardonable deed, and each hour deepened his misery. His conscience was exceedingly active; he had sinned against God and man; there could be no escape for such as he.

Dr. George Truett, the famous preacher, told of a man who said: "Dr. Truett, when you first came to town, I heard you preach every Sunday, and would have to hold on to my seat not to respond to your invitation. After the service I walked the streets for hours. I was miserable. I promised myself that I would respond the following Sunday, but when the invitation hymn was sung, I froze! I could not step out into the aisle. Dr. Truett, I know that you are a better preacher today than you were then, but when I hear you preach, I no longer feel as I once did. Has something happened to me?"

When the preacher told his story, he said: "I did not have the heart to tell him there is a line unseen by men, and when it is crossed, a thick barrier is formed, and you will never let Jesus in." Reproduced in part from *The Encyclopedia of 7700 Illustrations*, Paul Lee Tan, Assurance Publishers, Rockville, Maryland.

Judas . . . *Who Regretted His Pact* (Matthew 27:3-5)

"Then Judas, which had betrayed him, when he saw that he was condemned, repented himself, and brought again the thirty pieces of silver to the chief priests and elders, Saying, I have sinned in that I have betrayed the innocent blood . . . and he cast down the pieces of silver in the temple, and went and hanged himself."

The body of Judas hanging at the end of a rope was one of the most pathetic sights in history. Yet, it was not the rope which killed the traitor; he was dead before he died! The warning signals which had troubled him throughout the ministry of Jesus had disappeared. That pitiable man had thrown away his last chance to love and serve the Savior. His final disheveled appearance before the members of the Sanhedrin would never be forgotten. His face was torn by anguish; his cheeks were wet with tears; and the coins for which he sacrificed the Lord were thrown on the floor. He had sold his Leader for the price of a slave.

Did that desperate man reminisce before placing the rope around his neck? Did he recall the many times he had spoken with Jesus? It should never be forgotten that Judas was an ordained minister. Even he could not forget the day when Christ commissioned him to preach the Gospel, and endued him with "power against unclean spirits, to cast them out, and to heal all manner of sickness and all manner of disease" (Matt. 10:1).

The following months were filled with happiness as he traveled from place to place with his colleagues announcing the kingdom of God was at hand. When he became treasurer of the party, his eyes shone with delight; Judas loved being important. Those were delightful days, but unfortunately growing pride and increasing ambition destroyed his soul.

It may never be known how often he ignored God's warnings. The traitor coveted the money placed in his care, but after he had stolen what he desired, he was probably elated. One mistake led to another, and finally the thief was confronted by his greatest temptation. He tried to console himself by believing Jesus had not lived up to expectation. The glittering kingdom about which so much had been said, was now a mirage. Judas began to compromise with the Lord's enemies, and that was the beginning of the end. "Then one of the twelve, called Judas Iscariot, went unto the chief priests, And said unto them, What will ye give me, and I will deliver him unto you? And they covenanted with him for thirty pieces of silver" (Matt. 26:14-15). That was the reimbursement money given to a slave owner if another man's ox inadvertently injured his slave (Exod. 21:21-32).

Judas sacrificed his soul upon an altar of greed. To obtain the highest price possible for the betrayal, he ignored the warnings of the Almighty. Finally when he was beyond redemption he felt some remorse, but he had reached a point of no return and was friendless. Alone in his misery, he decided to commit suicide. "He went out, and it was night" (John 13:30). Even in eternity Judas will remember the dastardly deed which ruined his character, destroyed his hopes and damned his soul (Luke 16:19-31).

Paul . . . *Who Resolved His Problems* . . . (1 Tim. 1:15-16)

". . . Christ Jesus came into the world to save sinners; of whom I am chief. Howbeit, for this cause I obtained mercy."

It was significant that Paul never forgot his earliest mistakes. Even when he was approaching the end of his career, he said: "I was a blasphemer, and a persecutor, and injurious" (1 Tim. 1:13). When given the opportunity to defend himself before the governor at Caesarea, the apostle said: "And herein do I exercise myself, to have always a conscience void of offence toward God and toward men" (Acts 24:16). To the best of his ability Paul avoided displeasing the Lord, and endeavored to live a life beyond reproach. Yet, although he tried hard to forget the attacks against the early Christians, he failed in his efforts. When he frowned it became evident that his conscience was still active. This was apparent when he wrote to the Romans saying: "I am carnal, sold under sin. For that which I do I allow not; For what I would, I do not, but what I hate, that I do" (Rom. 7:14-15).

God had pardoned Paul's earlier indiscretions, but the apostle had difficulty forgiving himself. That was one of his greatest problems. Nevertheless, he discovered a remedy for his ills, and found a way by which to escape the mental torment which could have interfered with his ministry. He said: "I obtained mercy, that in me first Jesus Christ might shew forth all long-suffering, for a pattern to them which should hereafter believe on him to life everlasting" (1 Tim. 1:16). Paul's intensity of service revealed the secret of his continual enjoyment. He was determined to please the Lord even more than he had formerly grieved Him. Effective service for Christ helped to minimize the accusations of his conscience. Some people are content merely to express regret for their failure; others never rest until they have at least tried to pay their debt. Paul would have agreed with Dr. Oswald J. Smith who wrote:

> There is joy in serving Jesus
> As I journey on my way:
> Joy that fills the heart with praises
> Every hour and every day.

THE PEOPLE WHO
DESIRED TO SEE JESUS

During his thrilling evangelistic crusades in Britain, Charles M. Alexander sang at a school for blind children. His renditions charmed the audience, but when he asked if any child had a special request, a small boy lifted a hand and replied: "Please sir, will you sing 'Never lose sight of Jesus'?" The lad was thrilled to hear his favorite hymn, but the light on his face brought tears to the singer's eyes. The scholar could not see the soloist, nor any person in the hall, but evidently he could see Jesus, and appreciated the words of Johnson Oatman who wrote:

> O pilgrim bound for the heavenly land,
> Never lose sight of Jesus.
> He'll lead you gently with loving hand,
> Never lose sight of Jesus.

The books of the New Testament offered excellent counsel to the Christians of the first century, but nothing superseded that which was given in the epistle to the Hebrews. The writer said: "Wherefore seeing we also are compassed about with so great a cloud of witnesses, let us lay aside every weight, and the sin which doth so easily beset us, and let us run with patience the race that is set before us, *looking unto Jesus* the author and finisher of our faith" (Heb. 12:1-2). It is never wise nor safe to cease looking at Christ. When Peter was invited by Jesus to walk upon the Sea of Galilee, he did not sink until he ceased looking at his Master. ". . . and when Peter was come down out of the ship, he walked on the water to go to Jesus. *But when he saw the wind boisterous*, he was afraid: and beginning to sink, he cried, saying, Lord save me" (Matt. 14:29-30). Christians are often surrounded by threatening storms of life, but the only way to walk triumphantly over the things which threaten, is to "never lose sight of Jesus." The New Testament tells of certain people who desired to see the Lord.

The Disturbed Philip . . . *Conferring* (John 12:20-22)

Philip was worried! The creases upon his brow indicated he had no idea what to do! A group of Gentiles had sought his aid, saying, "Sir, we would see Jesus," but the apostle knew he was confronted with a problem. Jesus and His followers were attending the feast at Jerusalem, and the Lord had been separated from the disciples. He had gone into the inner court of the temple where Gentiles were denied admittance. Greeks who had become proselytes were only allowed to enter the outer parts of the temple area.

The strangers were aware of the restrictions, but believed Philip could arrange an interview with the famous Man from Galilee. Probably their foreign garments indicated they were Gentiles, and their approach caused apprehension for the apostle. They were extremely courteous, but they were Gentiles; their presence could lead to serious repercussions in a place where they were not welcome.

Philip looked at the suppliants, but his thoughts were in a turmoil. He could not take them into a prohibited area, but would he be justified in asking the Lord to come out to meet them? What could he possibly do? Philip was a timid man who was never sure how to solve problems. Then he thought of his resourceful brother, and smiled. John wrote: "Philip cometh and telleth Andrew; and again Andrew and Philip tell Jesus" (John 12:22).

When the Lord heard about the request of the strangers, He said: "The hour is come that the Son of man should be glorified. Verily, verily, I say unto you, Except a corn of wheat fall into the ground and die, it abideth alone: but if it die, it bringeth forth much fruit" (John 12:23-24). The Lord's eyes were those of a seer, for beyond the small group He saw a large world of Gentiles waiting to hear the gospel. He knew the only way by which those nations could enter the kingdom of God would be through the redemptive work completed through His death.

The fact that Greeks (Gentiles) had come to Jerusalem to worship at a Jewish feast was exceedingly intriguing. Their countrymen had many gods, but were never sure if they had enough. They, therefore, erected an altar to the unknown god in case an offended deity should complain (Acts 17:23). The Greeks who met Philip had rejected their national faith to embrace

Judaism. Evidently their questions remained unanswered, and the quest for spiritual satisfaction continued.

After arriving in Jerusalem where all the benefits of their new religion could be enjoyed, they still searched for reality, and risked censure and criticism from Jewish leaders. It had become evident that Jesus of Nazareth was detested by the Sanhedrin, yet in spite of this fact the strangers deliberately sought Him. That fact was thought-provoking. They were about to discover the difference between religious legalism and a vital faith. Could the Nazarene teach them something they needed to know? If so, nothing should interfere with their desire to hear Him. They set an example for all nations. The wisest way to learn about God is to sit at the feet of His Son.

The Determined Publican . . . *Climbing* (Luke 19:3)

"And he (Zacchaeus) sought to see Jesus *who he was*; and could not for the press, because he was little of stature. And he ran before, and climbed up into a sycamore tree to see him: for he was to pass that way." Evidently, this tax-gatherer was completely different from the Greeks who met Philip in Jerusalem. They had spent much time debating the pros and cons of comparative religions, and had finally decided that Judaism was better than idolatry.

On the other hand, Zacchaeus could not have cared less about any faith. Ecclesiastical matters were outside the circle of his interest. His god was money, and every day he worshiped at his self-made shrine.

The statement: "And he sought to see Jesus who he was" is interesting. After three and a half years of the most dynamic ministry ever known on earth, it would have been inconceivable that any resident of Palestine would have been unaware of the identity of Jesus. The Lord's message given to the disciples of John the Baptist explained what had transpired within the nation. ". . . Go your way, and tell John what things ye have seen and heard; how that the blind see, the lame walk, the lepers are cleansed, the deaf hear, the dead are raised, to the poor the gospel is preached . . ." (Luke 7:22-23).

With this kind of thing happening month after month, it

would have been impossible for Zacchaeus *not to know who Jesus was*! The text must therefore mean that the tax-gatherer climbed a tree to see which of the party was its leader. Zacchaeus had not done this earlier. What he had heard may have caused a measure of interest, but it was not sufficient to generate concern and a desire to meet the Healer.

Jericho was situated in one of the most fertile parts of Palestine. It was on a main highway. The balm which came from the Gilead district was sent through the city and examined by the customs officials. It is believed the Roman authorities sold the franchise to Zacchaeus, who employed other tax-gatherers to share his responsibility. He remained the chief man in the business, and evidently had become wealthy. Luke said: "And he was rich!" His testimony given later to Jesus caused endless discussion. "Behold, Lord, the half of my goods I give to the poor, and if I have taken anything from any man by false accusation, I restore him fourfold" (Luke 19:8).

Some teachers believe this had been the normal practice in the business affairs of the diminutive official. But, if that were the case, it would be difficult to explain the never-ceasing hatred of the people among whom he lived. They would have known whether or not he was a cheat, or an honest man trying to do his job. It may never be known which of the two interpretations is true, but at least we may be assured Zacchaeus resembled a multitude of men and women who live today.

Probably most people have heard of Jesus. The nations of the Western Hemisphere know about His mighty works, but unfortunately, many remain indifferent. They are only interested in trying to survive in a materialistic world. The Greeks who came to Philip were still seeking something greater than what they possessed. Zacchaeus was apparently moved by curiosity, which made him climb a tree to see the Lord.

The Doubtful Preacher . . . *Coming* (John 3:2)

When overwhelming problems arise, it is wise to seek advice from an excellent counselor. It was this fact which brought Nicodemus to Jesus of Nazareth; his mind had been challenged by incontrovertible facts. The ruler of the synagogue was an excellent student of the scripture and was aware that a very important prediction had been made by the prophet Daniel. "Know therefore and understand, that from the going forth of the commandment to restore and to build Jerusalem unto the Messiah the Prince shall be seven weeks, and threescore and two weeks: the street shall be built again, and the wall even in troublous times. And after three score and two weeks shall Messiah be cut off, but not for himself . . ." (Dan. 9:25-26). Nicodemus knew the predicted time had elapsed, and if there were any truth in the prophet's utterances, the Messiah at that time was an adult.

Constantly, the questions arose in his mind — "Can Jesus of Nazareth be our Messiah?" Every day he saw crowds hurrying to hear the new Teacher, and even from within his office he was able to hear the praises of people who had been healed. Evidently there was no other potential Messiah in the nation. If Jesus were the Messiah, the population should know about the fact. If He were not, the prophecies of Daniel were unreliable and foolish. That problem harassed the illustrious ruler, therefore, he "came to Jesus by night, and said unto him, Rabbi, we know that thou art a teacher come from God: for no man can do these miracles that thou doest, except God be with him" (John 3:2). That statement revealed his state of mind.

He asked no question; he gave no reason for the late night visit; and his speech ceased almost as quickly as it commenced. The man was embarrassed and nervous—but *he had come*—in spite of many reasons which could have kept him away. The Ruler was another religious man who believed his faith should be consistent. Nicodemus struggled with his problems and finally admitted his need to meet the Carpenter. A personal confrontation with the Son of God changed his life.

Had he refrained from obeying his instincts, Nicodemus would have been troubled and convicted throughout the rest of his career. There comes a time in the life of every person when problems arise and questions demand answers. Unfortunately many people are too proud to admit their need of help, and they fear adverse comments from neighbors and friends. When men are overwhelmed by spiritual difficulties, they consult a minis-

140

ter. It should never be forgotten that through the Scriptures it is still possible to interview Him Who said: "I am the way, the truth, and the life: no man cometh unto the Father, but by me" (John 14:6). No person should ever question the value of coming to Christ *until he has come*!

The Delighted People . . . *Confessing* (John 4:40-42)

The city of Sychar had been disturbed by the testimony of its most unpopular woman. Dignified ladies avoided her company, and men were afraid to be seen in her presence. She had an irresistible desire for male companionship, and was living with a man whom she had not married. Her attitude and disregard for decency offended the neighbors, but she remained unconcerned. Normally, that woman of Samaria avoided contact with critics, but on this particular day, her voice was heard echoing through the streets. She seemed beside herself as she told her story. She had met a Man Who was different from all others! "He told me all things that ever I did. Is not this the Christ?" (John 4:29). People stared in disbelief; ladies turned away; but the testimony intrigued everybody. Ultimately, ". . . they went out of the city and came unto him" (John 4:30). Evidently Christ was still at the well and as the people stood nearby, He began to preach. When the service terminated, the people said to the woman: "Now we believe, not because of thy saying, for we have heard him ourselves, and know that this is indeed the Christ, the Savior of the world" (John 4:42).

The greatest annual attraction in Ancient Corinth was the Isthmian Games, where huge crowds gathered to witness the various events. The favorite spectacle was the relay race, where teams of young athletes carried a lighted torch, which at interval, was passed to a fellow member of the team. The Greeks added a special phase to their language. "Let those who have the light pass it on." The woman whom Jesus met at Sychar's well was a great example of that truth. As soon as she possessed the light, she passed it on to the citizens of Sychar, and became one of the first female evangelists.

The Greeks came to Philip and Jesus because they realized something was lacking in their religious experiences. Zacchaeus was suddenly awakened to the fact that throughout his life he had definitely missed something. Nicodemus came because it was the only logical thing to do; he needed information. The people of Sychar responded because they had been stirred by the testimony of a woman. People who dig to find water are very foolish if a fountain of living water is springing up before their eyes. The Savior said: "Come unto me . . . and I will give you rest" (Matt. 11:28). The only way to discover His ability to fulfill that promise — is to *come*!

Tom Wallace, the well-known preacher, admits his favorite illustration about happiness comes from his own ministry. At the commencement of a Sunday morning service at the Bible Baptist Church in Elkton, Maryland, a stranger entered the church and seemed to be amazed at the large congregation.

Tom tells the story: "He came down the aisle and sat in the second row from the front. As the sermon proceeded he listened with the utmost attention, and was one of the first to respond to the invitation to trust Christ. His hand waved back and forth continually as if he were afraid it would not be seen. He stood stiff and erect when I asked if he would like to be saved; if he believed that Christ died for him. His eyes were gleaming when he responded: 'Yes, Sir, I want to do just that.' When he came into the baptistry, I gently lowered him into the water, and then lifted him to walk in newness of life. Suddenly, he began to clap his hands as he shouted 'Hot dog; hot dog; hot dog.' My people roared with laughter, but I reminded them the man was not accustomed to amens, praise the Lord, and hallelujahs. He was praising the Lord in the only vocabulary he knew."

Expressions of joy are the language of the soul; the greatest anomaly in the world is an unhappy Christian! Certain scriptures relate to this fact.

The Joy of Acceptance (Acts 8:38-39)

"And he commanded the chariot to stand still: and they went down both into the water, both Philip and the eunuch; and he baptized him. And when they were come up out of the water, the Spirit of the Lord caught away Philip, that the eunuch saw him no more; *and he went on his way rejoicing*."

This was one of the earliest missionary triumphs of the Christian church. The final commission given by the Savior was: "Go ye into all the world, and preach the gospel to every creature" (Mark 16:15). Yet, even before the disciples could obey that command, the Lord was preparing the way for the dissemination of His message. A high-ranking official from Ethiopia, who was either a convert to Judaism or a Jew of the dispersion, had been to a feast in Jerusalem. He was returning to his home in North Africa when a stranger approached his chariot. Philip had been preaching in Samaria, but the Holy Spirit commanded him to leave the evangelistic meetings. He said: " . . . Arise, and go toward the south unto the way that goeth down from Jerusalem unto Gaza, which is desert. And he arose and went: and, behold, a man of Ethiopia, an eunuch of great authority under Candace queen of the Ethiopians, who had the charge of all her treasure, and had come to Jerusalem for to worship, Was returning, and sitting in his chariot read Esaias the prophet" (Acts 8:26-28).

Probably Philip was extremely surprised when he was told to leave Samaria, for his services in that area were the greatest since Pentecost. Luke wrote: "Then Philip went down to the city of Samaria, and preached Christ unto them. And the people with one accord gave heed unto . . . Philip . . . hearing and seeing the miracles which he did. For unclean spirits, crying with loud voice, came out of many that were possessed with them: and many taken with palsies, and that were lame, were healed. And there was great joy in that city" (Acts 8:5-8). To most observers it was a mistake to leave the overwhelming possibilities among the Samaritan people. It would be interesting to know what Philip thought at that time.

The evangelist's subsequent meeting with the official from Ethiopia, and how that convert became the first missionary to North Africa is known throughout the world. Philip had reached a *city* in Samaria, but through the convert in the desert, he influenced a *continent*. Religion brought the man to Jerusalem, but Christ returned with him to Ethiopia.

It is significant that North Africa became one of the strongholds of the Christian faith during the second century. The eunuch, who only met the preacher once, returned to his home to evangelize his people. Although his spiritual advisor was suddenly removed, the convert *"went on his way rejoicing."* His friend explained the scriptures, and introduced him to fellowship with the Lord. All the money he controlled was nothing compared with the treasure within his soul.

The Joy of Assurance (Luke 10:17-20)

"And the seventy returned again with joy, saying, Lord, even the devils are subject unto us through thy name. And he said unto them . . . Notwithstanding in this rejoice not, that the spirits are subject unto you; *but rather rejoice, because your names are written in heaven.*"

The disciples were ecstatic! They had just completed their first evangelistic tour, and the results exceeded their expectations. They had often watched and admired their Master but on those occasions Jesus assumed responsibility for everything that happened. They had no worries and very little care. This tour had been different; they were on their own! Whatever fears filled their souls were dispelled by the success of their mission. When they returned, they gave their glowing report and assured Jesus everything had been satisfactory. Even the evil spirits had been forced to obey their commands. Modern evangelists would have claimed the closing of hospitals, doctors with little to do, and police without prisoners! Throughout their itinerary the disciples experienced continuing victory, and they were elated.

"And Jesus said unto them . . . in this rejoice not, that the spirits are subject unto you; but rather rejoice, because your names are written in heaven. . . . And he turned him unto his disciples, and said privately, Blessed are the eyes which see the things that ye see: For I tell you, that many prophets and kings have desired to see those things which ye see, and have not seen them; and to hear those things which ye hear, and have not heard them" (Luke 10:20-24).

It was thought-provoking that those ordinary, uneducated fishermen possessed treasure of incalculable worth. The combined wisdom of Solomon, wealth of David, and knowledge of the prophets could not provide the happiness which the disciples possessed. The writer to the Hebrews, referring to the saints of earlier times, said, "And these all, having obtained a good report through faith, received not the promise: God having provided some better thing for us, that they without us should not be made perfect" (Heb. 11:30-40).

The followers of Jesus were not always sure where they would sleep at night, and there were occasions when their future appeared bleak. They had left their homes, and no longer had a regular income. Yet God knew them by name; He watched their progress, and had given orders their names were to be indelibly inscribed in His book of life. Christ had promised nothing in time or eternity would pluck them from the Father's hand (John 10:28-29). That was a cause for continuing thanksgiving.

The Joy of Assembling (Acts 11:22-24)

"Then tidings of these things came unto the ears of the church which was in Jerusalem; and they sent forth Barnabas, that he should go as far as Antioch, Who, when he came, and had seen the grace of God, *was glad*, and exhorted them all, that with purpose of heart they would cleave unto the Lord. For he was a good man, and full of the Holy Ghost and of faith: and much people was added unto the Lord."

The church was growing daily; the testimony of the preachers was irresistible, and wherever the persecuted brethren went, people were formed into assemblies. Revival was spreading through the land, and it was to be expected the apostles in Jerusalem would become aware of the current events. Denominations were unknown; the converts were united in fellowship with Christ, and each belonged to the others.

The apostles were delighted with the news, and they sent Barnabas to investigate and encourage the preachers in the provinces. He accepted the assignment, and eventually arrived in Antioch. The people's efforts to win lost souls were outstanding, and their dedication was easily discerned. The visitor from Jerusalem was stirred and his appreciation was evident. "He was glad, and exhorted them all, that with purpose of heart, they would cleave unto the Lord."

Palestine was well known for its religious and political arguments, and it was thrilling for Barnabas to see how strangers, through faith in Christ, were becoming children of God. Furthermore, it was obvious these people enjoyed church fellowship; they worshiped harmoniously together, singing psalms and hymns. When the need arose, they gave money that other Christians might overcome financial problems. The power of the love of Christ was astonishing, for converts continued to help each other. Many years later when Paul was aware of similar circumstances, he wrote to the Corinthian church to describe what had happened in the churches of Macedonia. "How that in a great trial of affliction *the abundance of their joy* and their deep poverty abounded unto the riches of their liberality" (2 Cor. 8:2).

A Christian who knows nothing of fellowship with others becomes a religious hermit. A man or woman who refuses contact with other people becomes a recluse deprived of the joy of winning souls for Christ. The early Christians valued fellowship with other believers and consequently, the writer to the Hebrews said: "And let us consider one another to provoke unto love and to good works. *Not forsaking the assembling of yourselves together*, as the manner of some is . . ." (Heb. 10:24-25). The Christian church is the home of the believer; a man without a home can easily become a hobo!

The Joy of Adoration (John 20:19-20)

"Then the same day at evening, being the first day of the week, when the doors were shut where the disciples were assembled for fear of the Jews, came Jesus and stood in the midst, and saith unto them, Peace be unto you. And when he had so said, he shewed unto them his hands and his side. *Then were the disciples glad, when they saw the Lord.*"

Webster's dictionary defines adoration as "*the homage paid to one in high esteem, profound reverence, great love and respect; to love greatly.*" It would be very difficult to describe the emotions of the disciples when they saw the risen Lord. Their night of frustration and anguish had been long and bitter; their greatest hopes remained unfulfilled; all for which they had hoped and worked had ended in failure. Then came the resurrection when the astonished disciples saw with awe and wonder the face of their Lord.

They had considered the teaching of the Sadducees who believed death was terminal. The reappearance of Jesus proved they were mistaken. Christ was the greatest of all teachers, for He had announced correctly what would happen. He predicted His death, burial and resurrection, and had accomplished that which was promised. His appearance assured them He would always be accessible, and gave new meaning to His promise, "I will never leave you nor forsake you."

The closed door of the room in which they sat indicated terror had gripped their souls; they feared the possibility of capture and punishment. Yet, when they saw the wound-prints in the Savior's outstretched hands, their fear vanished. Perhaps they did not fully comprehend what had happened, but the fact that He was standing before them was all they needed. They worshiped Him, and joy began to change their outlook. There was no need to anticipate heaven; it had arrived! They enjoyed preaching the gospel and sharing companionship, but previous experiences became insignificant when they sat at His feet. Later when they met on the beach, it mattered not whether He preached or performed miracles, it was sufficient to see and worship Him. Jesus was "the altogether lovely one."

The Greek word "*chairo*" is used in all these references, and indicates that joy is a chief characteristic of the Christian life. Dr. Thayer states the word means "*to rejoice exceedingly.*" It is not difficult to appreciate the stranger's thrilling exclamation when the joy of the Lord flooded his soul. Perhaps even the angels laughed when the man shouted: "Hot dog; hot dog, hot dog." There might be a veiled connection between the aforementioned scriptures and the statement in Luke 19:37-40. "And when he was come nigh, even now at the descent of the mount of Olives, the whole multitude of the disciples began to rejoice and praise God with a loud voice for all the mighty works that they had seen; Saying, Blessed be the King that cometh in the name of the Lord: peace in heaven, and glory in the highest. Ans some of the Pharisees from among the multitude said unto him, Master, rebuke thy disciples. And he answered and said unto them, I tell you that, if these should hold their peace, the stones would immediately cry out." Oswald J. Smith was correct when he wrote:

> There is joy, joy, joy in serving Jesus
> Joy that throbs within my heart.
> Every moment, every hour,
> As I draw upon His power,
> There is joy, joy, joy that never will depart.

THE BENDS IN GOD'S ROADS!

One of the little-big words of the Bible is the conjunction,— *but*. Dr. Strong, in his concordance, mentions nearly four thousand places where it can be found. The word signifies a change of direction, and represents a possibility after a conclusion. A matter may be considered finalized, and then someone either says or writes — *but*. It represents a bend in a highway where new vistas of beauty come into view. Paul and other writers recognized this fact, and added another word — *but God*! This statement frequently expresses an intervention of the grace of God, when seemingly impossible things become possible.

Stephen, the first martyr of the church, provided a glorious example of this fact. Addressing the religious leaders of his generation, he referred to the story of Joseph, and said: "And the patriarchs moved with envy, sold Joseph into Egypt: *but God* was with him. And delivered him out of all his afflictions . . ." (Acts 7:9-10). An apparent tragedy was turned into a glorious triumph, for Jehovah overruled in the affairs of nations, and provided help which otherwise would have been denied. Luke also wrote: "And he (the rich man) said . . . I will pull down my barns, and build greater; and there will I bestow all my fruits and my goods. And I will say to my soul, Soul, thou hast much goods laid up for many years; take thine ease, eat, drink, and be merry. *But God* said unto him, Thou fool, this night thy soul shall be required of thee: then whose shall those things be, which thou hast provided?" (Luke 12:18-20). At least five examples can be found which suggest the apostle Paul used this method to emphasize truth.

The "But God" of Objection

"But the Lord said unto him, Go thy way: for he is a chosen vessel unto me, to bear my name before the Gentiles, and kings, and the children of Israel" (Acts 9:15). Throughout his ministry, Paul never ceased to be amazed at the miraculous way in which he had been brought to Christ. A persecutor had become a preacher; a murderer had been transformed into a minister.

The key to the miracle of grace was the intervening mercy of

149

God when Ananias was reluctant to obey the commandment of the Lord. The evil reputation of Saul of Tarsus had terrorized the entire church and his deadly mission to apprehend the saints in Damascus filled every believer with dread. When Ananias was told to visit the notorious persecutor, he replied: "Lord, I have heard by many of this man, how much evil he hath done to thy saints at Jerusalem: And here he hath authority from the chief priests to bind all that call upon thy name" (Acts 9:13-14).

Paul understood the fear which gripped the soul of Ananias, but if the saint remained in isolation, irreparable harm would have been done. "*But God* said unto him . . ." The Lord's intervention supplied the necessary courage, and proceeding on his way, Ananias met the persecutor and said: "Brother Saul, the Lord, even Jesus . . . hath sent me . . ." (Acts 9:17). All Christians agree that without the grace of God, few, if any, would ever have met the Savior.

The "But God" of Opportunity

The early church was established in a world which professed to be exceedingly wise. Grecian culture had penetrated into all countries, and at Athens, philosophers gathered daily on Mars Hill to hear new doctrines. The Jews valued the writings of their ancestors, and claimed their knowledge superseded that of all nations. The Romans possessed many skills, and evidence of their prowess can still be seen throughout Europe. They worshiped many gods; the Jews worshiped Jehovah, and the Greeks had so many idols they were fearful of having forgotten one (Acts 17:23).

Paul's message seemed ludicrous; many of his scholarly listeners scoffed when he claimed a Carpenter was the Creator of the world. They were critical when he claimed the blood of a malefactor could wash away guilt. Yet, when Paul wrote his first letter to the Corinthian church, he made an important announcement. "But we speak the wisdom of God . . . Which none of the princes of this world knew: for had they known it, they would not have crucified the Lord of glory. But as it is written, Eye hath not seen, nor ear heard, neither have entered into the heart of man, the things which God hath prepared for them that love him. *But God* hath revealed them unto us by his Spirit . . . Now we have received, not the spirit of the world, but the Spirit which is of God; that we might know the things that are freely given to us of God" (1 Cor. 2:7-12). Paul claimed his doctrines were of more importance than the culture, education and traditions taught throughout his world. God had revealed eternal truth, which enabled foolish people to become extremely wise.

The "But God" of Omnipotence

Paul was the greatest preacher in the early church, and it is thought-provoking to discover his theme was always the death and resurrection of Christ. He never deviated from his methods of instruction. If the actions of men could be compared with a highway, then it was evident the road led to nowhere until God performed a miracle. Paul said: "And though they found no cause of death in him (Jesus), yet desired they Pilate that he should be slain. And when they had fulfilled all that was written of him, they took him down from the tree, and laid him in a sepulchre. . . ." At that precise moment in time, the faith of the disciples had been shattered; their work was in jeopardy; their future bleak. Plans for an earthly kingdom of God were seemingly destroyed—"*But God* raised Christ from the dead . . ." (Acts 13:28-30). When men believed the Carpenter would never again trouble the nation, the power of the Almighty was manifested, and Jesus was raised from the dead — never more to die. Paul insisted this was true, and his ministry emphasized the Savior was alive.

The "But God" of Outreach

The city of Ephesus was one of the most vile cities in the world. It was the headquarters for demon worship and idolatry, and even today in the remains of that once illustrious city, is an announcement engraved in stone, advertising that prostitution was free within the temple precincts. The missionary had entered that cesspool of iniquity to preach the gospel, and his work had been very successful. A church was established, and Paul was its pastor for a considerable length of time (Acts

19:10). That assembly became one of the greatest of all churches, but Paul never permitted the members to forget whence they had come.

He wrote: ". . . in time past ye walked according to the course of this world, according to the prince of the power of the air, the spirit that now worketh in the children of disobedience: Among whom also we all had our conversation in times past in the lusts of our flesh, fulfilling the desires of the flesh and of the mind; and were by nature the children of wrath, even as others . . ." It was impossible to misunderstand the apostle's message; his words were challenging and destroyed any pride which readers had in their former associations. Paul insisted they were exceptionally guilty—"*But God,* who is rich in mercy, for his great love wherewith he loved us, Even when we were dead in sins, hath quickened us together with Christ, (by grace ye are saved)" (Eph. 2:2-5). The unconverted people of Ephesus had walked along a road which went deeper into darkness, but suddenly, there had been a bend in the highway, and as the converts proceeded, they saw a sunrise, and a hill upon which stood a cross.

The "But God" of Overcoming

When he wrote to the Philippians, Paul said: "But I trust in the Lord that I also myself shall come shortly. Yet I supposed it necessary to send Epaphroditus, my brother, and companion in labour, and fellow-soldier, but your messenger, and he that ministered to my wants. For he longed after you all, and was full of heaviness, because ye had heard that he had been sick. For indeed he was sick nigh unto death: *But God* had mercy on him; and not on him only, but on me also, lest I should have sorrow upon sorrow. I sent him therefore the more carefully . . ." (Phil. 2:24-28).

It is refreshing to read that although many sick people were healed during Paul's ministry, at other times, for reasons unknown, he was unable to heal his dearest friends. It is misleading and erroneous to teach all sickness is the result of sin. Sometimes the Lord permits things to happen to increase our spiritual growth. It had been necessary to leave Trophimus at

Miletum where he had become gravely ill (2 Tim. 4:20). The apostle recognized it would be unwise to permit the sick member of his party to leave the island, and the brother was probably left in the care of a local Christian.

A similar event happened with Epaphroditus, the courier of the Philippian church. He had become gravely ill and apparently the intercession of Paul had been of no avail. The news of this sickness reached Philippi and caused great concern among the church members. It may therefore be assumed the illness had lasted a considerable time. Paul was worried; it appeared his friend was about to die. *"But God had mercy on him."* That simple statement is a window through which much may be seen. It is better to pray than to pout; wiser to be grateful than to grumble. Perhaps those words were written to remind all Christians that God knows about our problems, and in His own time will intervene on our behalf.

WHEN PAUL MADE UP HIS MIND!
(ACTS 17:22-23; 1 COR. 2:1-2)

Athens is one of the most attractive and fascinating cities in the world. There, in the shadow of the great Acropolis, a dreamer can see again the grandeur of ancient Greece. If Rome symbolized military might, Athens was famous for its intellectual excellence. Within the city were many schools, colleges and academies where some of the greatest scholars shared their knowledge with eager students. Dr. Frederic W. Farrar wrote: "It was full of professors, rhetors, tutors, arguers, discourcers, lecturers, grammarians, pedagogues, and gymnasts of every kind; and among all these . . . there was not one who displayed the least particle of originality or force. Conforming sceptics lived in hypocritical union with atheistic priests, and there was not even sufficient earnestness to arouse any antagonism between the empty negations of a verbal philosophy, and the hollow professions of a dead religion" (*The Life and Work of St. Paul*, page 303, published by Cassell and Company, London, 1897).

Athens, the center of philosophical brilliance, attracted scholars from many countries, and these people spent most of their time on Mars' Hill, just beneath the Acropolis. When I first visited this historic place, a wooden stairway had been built by the city, and it was easy to climb to the top of the small hill where ancient thinkers held their daily discussions. Unfortunately the weather and time destroyed that construction, and today tourists must climb the side of the hill. Nearly two thousand years ago, Paul carefully ascended those same steps and joined the scholars who apparently had nothing better to do than wait for a new speaker to expound his doctrine.

The apostle had just been in the nearby metropolis and was remembering its many altars. He knew the city was completely dominated by religion, and he had seen on street corners, in specially made alcoves, and upon every civic building, idols which eloquently testified to the faith of the Athenian people. He had been intrigued by one altar upon which was the inscription—*To the Unknown God*. Paul recognized the uncertainty of the people who had erected that idol. Evidently, they feared they had forgotten one deity, and to avert his possible wrath, they made an altar to inform him of their good intentions. Paul smiled and proceeded to address his illustrious audience.

What happened that day can never be forgotten. The listeners were pagans with little if any knowledge of Christianity. The apostle probably believed they would be incapable of understanding how death could lead to life; how the precious blood of Jesus was the only means by which sin could be forgiven. Writing to the Corinthians, Paul explained that the preaching of the cross was "unto the Greeks foolishness" (1 Cor. 1:23). Convinced that his usual approach would be ineffective, he proceeded to use the strange inscription as a means by which to reveal the "unknown god." Many teachers applaud his effort as evidence of psychological genius, but their opinion may be misleading.

His Great Discourse . . . *How Striking*

When Luke recorded the events of that memorable day, he condensed Paul's speech into ten verses which can be read in two minutes. It is evident that Paul said much more than was written by his friend. Even the short but difficult climb demanded a greater effort than is apparent from the record in the scripture. Perhaps Luke only wrote that which he considered worth remembering!

Paul spoke about the Creator, the nations of the world, the uselessness of man-made idols, and the fact of being judged in eternity. Exponents of any pagan religion could have supplied more information. Concluding his speech, Paul spoke of the resurrection, but he never mentioned the redeeming death of the Son of God. Luke said: "And when they heard of the resurrection of the dead, some mocked, and others said, We will hear thee again of this matter" (Acts 17:32). That resolve was never fulfilled, for when the arguments began Paul departed.

A few people were impressed either by what was said or by the appearance and eloquence of the speaker. As far as is known, they were the only signs of success attending Paul's efforts. He never established a church in Athens, and no letter was ever sent by him to saints residing within the city. Eventually the apostle wrote nine letters to churches, but unfortunately Athens was not on his list. If the establishing of an assembly be considered evidence of victory, then at Athens Paul failed in his mission.

His message appealed to the intellects of his hearers, but failed to stir their souls. He had preached of a Christ without His cross, and told of a day of judgment without explaining how a sinner might be justified. This was an admirable oration, but it was unimpressive—he had left the mainspring out of his watch! (See the author's book *Bible Treasures*, pgs. 131-132, published by Kregel Publications, Grand Rapids, Michigan.)

His Great Discovery . . . *How Startling*

"*After these things Paul departed from Athens, and came to Corinth*" (Acts 18:1). "There were two ways by which he could have traveled. Corinth was approximately forty miles from Athens, and it would have taken him two days to reach his objective. If, as has been conjectured, the apostle was not in good health, he might have decided to go by sea. In that case, the voyage would have taken five hours or more, according to weather conditions. The overland route would have led him into the city; the journey by sea would have taken him into a small port from which he would have walked a few miles to reach his destination. At that moment, not even Paul could have known the importance of his visit; he was about to face the greatest challenge of his life" (quoted from the author's commentary on *The Amazing Acts*, page 308, Kregel Publications, Grand Rapids, MI).

Whichever way he traveled, Paul had time for reflection. His memories of the visit to Athens could not have been pleasant; he was disappointed. The Greek metropolis was one of the few cities in which he never established a church. All pastors and evangelists have been despondent after preaching in a disappointing service. Then, sleep becomes elusive, and regret overwhelms the soul. It is significant that all the prophets were acquainted with that experience. As Paul either walked or sailed toward Corinth, he remembered his preaching before the Greek philosophers. He had quoted from the writings of their poets, but had said little about the words of his Lord. He produced arguments, but no conviction. His message had been woefully inadequate; its reasoning might have appeared attractive, but sermons which never mentioned the death of the Redeemer could not save souls nor establish assemblies.

This fact needs to be emphasized in our modern world. Some institutions, which unfortunately are called churches, teach that Jesus was the victim of a Jewish mob; that He was a good man who, regretfully, was crucified. Others are content to teach that the death of Jesus merely provided an excellent example for sufferers; He accepted what happened, and refused to strike His persecutors. They assert that if nations followed His example, wars would be unknown. The early Christians believed and taught that Christ died for the ungodly; that He bore the sins of many; that through His redeeming death eternal redemption was made possible for guilty sinners. That was the message which overcame empires, provided peace for convicted souls, and salvation for men and women. It remains an indisputable fact that each time revival brought new life to the church and renewal to decadent generations, that same Gospel was the message used and blessed by God. Paul wrote to the Roman Christians saying: "For I am not ashamed of the gospel of Christ: for it is the power of God unto salvation to every one that believeth; to the Jew first, and also to the Greek" (Rom. 1:16).

His Great Determination . . . *How Suggestive*

Athens was famous for its educational advantages and rhetorical persuasiveness; Corinth was infamous for its immorality. The Athenians had plenty of time to listen to visiting speakers; the citizens of Corinth had no time except to increase their wealth and exploit their sexual capabilities. The apostle knew he was about to confront a different type of audience, but as he approached the city, a great resolve filled his soul. It is significant that long afterward, when writing to the Corinthian church, he said: "And I, brethren, when I came to you, came not with excellency of speech or of wisdom, declaring unto you the testimony of God. For *I determined* not to know any thing among you, save Jesus Christ, and him crucified" (1 Cor. 2:1-2). The apostle never repeated the mistake made on Mars' Hill. The statement: "For I determined not to know anything among you" as supplied by the Amplified New Testament, is interesting. "For I resolved to know nothing—to be acquainted with (nothing), to make a display of the knowledge of (nothing), and to be conscious of (nothing)—among you except Jesus Christ, the Messiah, and Him crucified." The apostle was so disgusted with himself that even his self-criticism helped formulate the resolve that henceforth he would only preach the gospel. Great speakers of later generations shared his conviction.

Dr. F. M. Barton tells the story of a young minister who had spoken before a very old pastor. After the service he asked the older man: "What did you think of my sermon?" The answer was quickly forthcoming: "It was a very poor sermon — there was no Christ in it." The young man replied: "Well, Christ was not in the text; we are not to be preaching Christ always; we must preach what is in the text." The old saint responded: "Don't you know, young man, that from every town, village and hamlet in England, wherever it may be, there is a road to London. And from each text in the Scripture, there is a way that leads to the great metropolis of the Bible — Christ. My dear young brother, whenever you get a text, your business is to say: 'Now, how does that lead to Christ?' and then preach a sermon which leads to the great metropolis — Christ. I have not yet found a text that hasn't a road to the Savior in it. *If I should, I would make one.* I would go over hedge and ditch, but I would get to my Master for a sermon cannot do any good unless Christ is in it" (quoted from *One Hundred Great Texts, and Their Treatment*, F. M. Barton, 1914, published by Richard R. Smith, Inc., New York, 1930).

His Great Delight . . . *How Sublime*

"After these things Paul departed from Athens, and came to Corinth . . . And he reasoned in the synagogue every sabbath, and persuaded the Jews and the Greeks . . . and testified to the Jews that Jesus was Christ . . . And Crispus, *the chief ruler of the synagogue*, believed on the Lord with all his house; and many of the Corinthians hearing believed, and were baptized" (Acts 18:4-8). The conversion of that important Jewish citizen had far reaching repercussions. Eighteen months later, *when another chief ruler had been appointed*, Paul was brought before the judgment seat where Gallio, the judge, interrupted the trial by saying: "If it were a matter of wrong or wicked lewdness, O ye Jews, reason would that I should bear with you, But if it be a question of words and names, and of your law, look ye to it; for I will be no judge of such matters. And he drave them from the judgment seat. Then all the Greeks took Sosthenes, *the chief ruler of the synagogue*, and beat him before the judgment seat. And Gallio cared for none of those things" (Acts 18:14-17). Every citizen in Corinth knew Sosthenes, but few sympathized with him.

It is interesting to discover that later in his ministry, the apostle mentioned this man. Writing to the Christians in Corinth, the apostle said: "Paul, called to be an apostle of Jesus Christ through the will of God, and *Sosthenes our brother*" (1 Cor. 1:1). It is impossible to state all the details of the man's conversion to Christianity, but evidently someone had explained the gospel to him and probably Paul was that preacher.

After his beating by the mob, Sosthenes was a sick man, but one day the man whom he had persecuted called to see his accuser, and the visit led to great things. Sosthenes not only became a Christian — he became a fellow worker, and was with Paul when the Corinthian letter was written in Philippi. Two very important men who held high office in Corinth were won for Christ, and when Paul left the city, a thriving church had been established. Afterward, Paul said: "But God forbid that I should glory, save in the cross of our Lord Jesus Christ, by whom the world is crucified unto me, and I unto the world" (Gal. 6:14).

THE MAN WHO WAS READY! (ROMANS 1:15)

When General Eisenhower lay seriously ill in the Walter Reed Hospital in Washington, D.C., Billy Graham was invited to visit the dying President. He was told by the medical authorities that his visit could only last thirty minutes. When he entered the room the General greeted him with his customary smile, even though he realized he had not long to live.

Later, the preacher revealed what had taken place during that last conversation. At the end of the specified time the sick man asked the evangelist to lengthen his stay, and then said: "Billy, I want you to tell me again, how can I be sure my sins are forgiven, and that I am going to Heaven? Nothing else matters now."

"I took my New Testament and read scriptures to him. I pointed out that we are not going to Heaven because of our good works, nor because of money we have given to the church. We are going to Heaven totally and completely on the basis of the merits of what Christ did on the cross. Therefore he could rest in the comfort that Jesus paid it all. After prayer, Ike said: 'Thank you, I'm ready."

It is regrettable that many informed people cannot repeat the late President's statement. Luke described the reactions of three men who had the opportunity to become followers of Christ. The enthusiasm of the first man waned when he heard the Lord saying: "Foxes have holes, and birds of the air have nests; but the Son of man hath not where to lay his head." A warm comfortable bed at night was more attractive than lying beneath a hedge.

The second man did not have much interest in discipleship, and he made his family duties the excuse for avoiding acceptance of a new way of living. He might be ready — some day!

The third fellow wished to rejoin his family who, undoubtedly, would endeavor to dissuade him from starting something which would, in their estimation, interfere with his life. In any case, he would not do anything until he had basked in the warmth of his family's admiration. While the men considered other possibilities, their opportunity was possibly lost forever

(Luke 9:57-62). All three might have been ready — but other projects appeared to be more important.

Compared with these men, Paul's example shone forth with unusual splendor. He was ready at all times, in any place, to do or be whatever the Lord desired. That was the outstanding characteristic of his ministry. Even when he was helpless on the Damascus road, he said: "Lord, what wilt thou have me to do?" Then, soon after his conversion to Christ, it was said of him: "He straightway preached Christ in the synagogues."

That readiness continued throughout his ministry. He grew accustomed to going from stall to stall in market places to speak to business men about the claims of his Savior; at other times he went "from house to house," and when someone opened a door, the apostle preached the Gospel. Confronted by philosophers on Mars Hill, he testified before them; when his ship was about to sink in a storm, he witnessed to the captain and crew of the vessel. When he reached a certain island and discovered the governor was seriously ill, he supplied what was needed. Imprisoned in Rome, he preached both inside and outside of his prison.

As long as he lived he never willingly lost an opportunity to tell the story of God's redeeming grace, and among his final statements was "Henceforth there is laid up for me a crown of righteousness, which the Lord, the righteous judge, shall give me . . ." (2 Tim. 4:8). Three tremendous texts invite examination.

"I am Ready to Preach the Gospel . . . at Rome also"
    — The Special Service

The setting of this text is extremely interesting. Paul had already traversed most of the known world, and had preached in many of the major cities of earth. Rome was the one exception. That fact was exploited by some of the apostle's enemies who suggested he was a coward. That metropolis was exceptionally sinful; the emperor claimed to be divine, and any person who challenged his authority was murdered. Men were literally skinned alive, and others were fed to ravenous beasts to provide entertainment for onlookers.

Within the city was a small but energetic church. How it was formed remains a mystery. Probably Jews from Rome had been at the feast of Pentecost, where some were converted to Christianity. They carried the message to their homes, and provided the first fruits of the Gospel within the imperial city. Later, when persecution scattered the earliest Christians, some of them could have fled to Rome to give needed assistance to the saints already there.

It became increasingly evident that Rome was a hostile city where Christians were threatened. If it be possible to understand the plight of the Jews in Hitler's Berlin, it might be easy to appreciate the danger of Christians in Rome. Many were burned at stakes in the emperor's gardens, and others died in the arena. It was therefore to be expected that some critics would exploit the situation and charge Paul with cowardice.

Paul knew what was being said, and to end the controversy, he sent a letter to the Christians in Rome to refute the allegations. He emphasized his readiness to preach in Rome. The *"Three I ams"* in the first chapter of his epistle are worthy of scrutiny. *"I am debtor; I am ready; I am not ashamed."* The threats of hardship were unimportant. He *had* to visit the city whether he liked it or not, for otherwise, his conscience would destroy his happiness. God had given to him a treasure to convey to his friends in Rome, and until he fulfilled his commitments he was a thief, *keeping for himself something which belonged to others!*

Furthermore, his Gospel was needed urgently by the citizens of Rome. None of its inhabitants were as dangerous and difficult as he had been prior to his conversion. If Christ could save Saul of Tarsus, He could do the same for arrogant Romans. Therefore, it had become a necessity to visit the brethren in the city of Nero. It has been claimed that people are saved to serve. Paul's life was an outstanding example of that fact.

"I am Ready . . . to Die at Jerusalem" (Acts 21:13)
— *The Suggested Suffering*

Paul was a determined man; if it were possible to tunnel through or climb over high mountains of difficulties, he never waited to go around them. It might be said that his strength was his weakness! The feast at Jerusalem was swiftly approaching, and the apostle was aware that vast multitudes of visitors would throng the city. If he were able to be present, he would probably reach half of Asia merely by preaching in a street! When he considered the amazing possibilities his heart began to sing! Possibly he consulted ship's captains to obtain an estimated day of arrival; he had corresponded with his friends about land arrangements, and at that time, being present at the feast was the only thought in his mind.

When his ship reached Tyre, in Syria, Paul went ashore "And finding disciples, we tarried there seven days; who said to Paul through the Spirit, that he should not go up to Jerusalem" (Acts 21:4). The apostle listened to the words of his friends but frowned when he was urged to change his plans. Their counsel was a dark cloud against the blue sky of personal desire. Good winds had helped him to arrive early, and thus he had time to spare. Fellowship with other Christians was most desirable, but why should their influence ruin his plans? Unfortunately he was unwise and failed to accept a command *given "through the Holy Spirit."* If he were influenced by that message, he would not only lose the greatest opportunity of his lifetime, but would encourage critics to repeat their allegations. The insistent warnings given by the brethren at Tyre were annoying; Paul was glad when he continued his voyage to Caesarea.

"And when we had finished our course from Tyre, we came to Ptolemais, and saluted the brethren, and abode with them one day." That, in all probability, was the time necessary to unload cargo at the port. "And the next day we that were of Paul's company departed, and came unto Caesarea: and we entered into the house of Philip the evangelist, which was one of the seven, and abode with him. And the same man had seven daughters, virgins, which did prophesy. And as we tarried there many days, there came down from Judaea a certain prophet, named Agabus. And when he was come unto us, he took Paul's girdle, and bound his own hands and feet, and said, Thus saith the Holy Ghost, So shall the Jews at Jerusalem bind the man that owneth this girdle, and shall deliver him into the hands of the Gentiles. And when we heard these things, both we, and they of that place, besought him not to go up to Jerusalem."

The discussion and arguments probably ruined Paul's stay with Philip. The statement *"they of that place"* meant Philip, his family, and all the local Christians. When Luke and Paul's companions agreed with them, the apostle was opposed by every person present. Yet as far as he was concerned, *they were all wrong!* His amazing strength became weakness. Unfortunately, he stepped out of the will of God, and during his two-year imprisonment in Jerusalem was a worried man. It would have been more rewarding preaching to multitudes than watching spiders spinning webs in the corner of his cell!

Paul's reply to the friends in Caesarea revealed nothing would interfere with his plans to attend the forthcoming feast — not even the Spirit-given command at Tyre; the message delivered by the prophet, nor the persuasion and reasoning of his personal physician, Dr. Luke. He said: "What mean ye to weep and to break mine heart? for I am ready not to be bound only, but also to die at Jerusalem for the name of the Lord Jesus . . ." (Acts 21:8-13).

It is difficult to avoid the conclusion that Paul made one of the greatest mistakes of his life. It would have been wonderful to die for the Lord Jesus — but only if that were the expressed will of God. Nevertheless, in fairness to the apostle, it must be emphasized his determination was the reason why he never quit. He finished his course while others lingered along life's highway.

"I am Ready to be Offered . . . Poured Out" (2 Tim. 4:6)
— *The Supreme Sacrifice*

Paul knew the end of his life was approaching as he sat alone in his prison cell in Rome. Most of his friends had either been sent to assigned tasks, or had retired to their homes in the imperial city. Frequently Dr. Luke visited the prison to minister to the needs of his friend. Ahead lay another meeting with Nero, and it seemed inevitable that the great missionary would be executed. There was no escape, but Paul was ready for his supreme sacrifice.

His last letter to Timothy was destined to find an abiding place in the affections of all Christians. He wrote: "For I am now ready to be offered, and the time of my departure is at hand. I have fought a good fight, I have finished my course, I have kept the faith: Henceforth there is laid up for me a crown of righteousness, which the Lord, the righteous judge, shall give me at that day: and not to me only, but unto all them also that love his appearing" (2 Tim. 4:6-8). The intrepid evangelist, who had fought so valiantly against evil, was ready to lay aside his armor, and kneel in the presence of his Master.

The word translated *offered* is *spindomai*, and is translated in *The Englishman's Greek Testament* as "*I am already being poured out.*" *The Amplified Version of the New Testament* translates the entire passage: "For I am already about to be sacrificed — my life is about to be poured out (as a drink offering); the time of my (spirit's) release (from the body) is at hand and I will soon be free." The reference to being "*poured out*" is interesting, for it evidently referred to the drink-offering which was an integral part of temple worship (Num. 15:1-10). A drink-offering was never shared by the priests; it was totally and completely poured out before God; that is, it was offered exclusively to Jehovah.

Paul realized this process had already begun. His life-flow was ebbing; he had only a limited time to remain on earth. His final sacrifice would give pleasure to his Lord and peace to himself. Furthermore, the apostle had neither regret nor complaint; he was happy to be going home! Probably, when he was led to the place of his execution, he could already hear the singing of the angels. He was ready!

During the reign of the notorious Roman emperor, Nero, there was a company of distinguished soldiers known as "*The Emperor's Wrestlers.*" They were drawn from every part of the empire, and represented the finest athletes of their generation. It was reported that when the army was sent to fight in Gaul, the bravery of these men exceeded all other combatants.

When Nero heard that some of his troops were becoming Christians, he dispatched orders to the leader, Vespasian, commanding the men be executed. The General asked his army:

165

"Are there any among you who cling to the faith of the Christians?" Instantly forty wrestlers stepped forward and saluted. Vespasian was shocked to discover so many valiant men had forsaken the faith of Rome, and urged the men to recant. He gave them until evening to change their faith.

That night, in the midst of a very severe winter, the men refused to abandon Christianity; they were stripped of their clothing and made to walk to the middle of an ice-covered lake. Vespasian said: "I am not willing that your comrades should shed your blood. I shall leave you to the mercy of the elements."

As they marched to their death, the men sang: "Forty wrestlers wrestling for Thee, O Christ, to win for Thee the victory and from Thee the victor's crown." Throughout the night, Vespasian sat at his campfire watching and listening as the song became more subdued. As the new day dawned, one exhausted soldier returned; he had renounced his faith. But then, faintly, but clearly, came the song: "Thirty-nine wrestlers wrestling for Thee O Christ, to win for Thee the victory, and from Thee the victor's crown." When the commander saw the desperate man at the fire, and heard the renewed song of the Christians, he removed his clothing, and walking upon the frozen lake cried: "Forty westlers wrestling for Thee, O Christ, to win for Thee the victory, and from Thee the victor's crown." He had reached the point of no return, and he was ready.

FIVE MEN WHO SAW LIGHT AT
THE END OF A TUNNEL . . . or the five J's

(ROMANS 8:28)

It is impossible to understand the greatness of this text without an appreciation of the man who wrote it. The apostle Paul overcame tremendous problems. It would have been easy to say "all things" worked together for his personal good had he lived constantly on the mountain top of success. Paul endured more for his faith than any other person. He wrote: ". . . in labors more abundant, in stripes above measure, in prisons more frequent, in deaths oft. Of the Jews five times received I forty stripes save one. Thrice was I beaten with rods, once was I stoned, thrice I suffered shipwreck, a night and a day I have been in the deep. In journeyings often, in perils of water, in perils of robbers, in perils by mine own countrymen, in perils by the heathen, in perils in the city, in perils in the wilderness, in perils in the sea, in perils among false brethren; In weariness and painfulness, in watchings often, in hunger and thirst, in fastings often, in cold and nakedness. Beside those things that are without, that which cometh upon me daily, the care of all the churches" (2 Cor. 11:23-28). After enduring unprecedented anguish, the indomitable missionary wrote: "And we know that *all things* work together for good to them that love God." The apostle did not say *some* things — "*all* things work together for good." That conclusion was almost incomprehensible. Paul never complained. He looked at the unpleasant experiences of his career and thanked God they were vehicles through which the Almighty sent His greatest benedictions. Blessed is the man who rejoices in tribulation. The Bible supplies excellent examples of men who could see in the dark!

Jacob . . . *From Poverty to Peace* (Gen. 28:16-17).

"And Jacob awaked out of his sleep, and he said, Surely the LORD is in this place: and I knew it not. And he was afraid, and said, How dreadful is this place! this is none other but the house of God, and this is the gate of heaven." Jacob was running away from his family and God, but he could not outrun the

167

Lord. Unfortunately, his sleep had been ruined by a vivid dream. Maybe his stony pillow contributed to his discomfort, for he saw angels ascending and descending on a ladder which reached to Heaven. He had not enjoyed the experience; he had a very guilty conscience. He realized that God could have killed him, but the fact Jacob was still alive indicated the Lord cared for him. He took his stony pillow and set it up as if it were an altar. Perhaps even the angels listened when he exclaimed: "If God will be with me, and keep me in this way that I go, and will give me bread to eat, and raiment to put on, So that I come again to my father's house in peace; then shall the LORD be my God" (Gen. 28:20-21). Ultimately, Jacob became a prince with God, but the beginning of his transformation came when he knelt at his first altar. He discovered the Lord could take mistakes and weave them into a fabric which would last eternally.

Joseph . . . *From the Pit to the Palace* (Psalm 105:17-22)

"He sent a man before them, even Joseph who was sold for a servant: whose feet they hurt with fetters; he was laid in iron; Until the time that his word came: the word of the LORD tried him. The king sent and loosed him; even the ruler of the people, and let him go free. He made him lord of his house, and ruler of all his substance."

When Joseph was placed in the pit and later sold to strangers, he probably believed he had been forsaken by everybody; even his brethren had betrayed him. That idea was drastically changed when he, ultimately, said to his brothers: "Now therefore be not grieved, nor angry with yourselves, that ye sold me hither: for God did send me before you to preserve life. God sent me before you to preserve you a posterity in the earth, and to save your lives by a great deliverance. So now it was not you that sent me hither, but God: and he hath made me a father to Pharaoh, and lord of all his house, and a ruler throughout all the land of Egypt" (Gen. 45:5, 6-8).

It was significant that Joseph did not enumerate the times of adversity through which he had passed; he never complained about the wife of Pharaoh, nor his imprisonment on false charges. He saw that all his clouds had silver linings, and would have endorsed Paul's idea that all things worked together for good to those who loved God.

Job . . . *Problems to Prosperity* (Job 23:8-10)

"Behold, I go forward, but he is not there; and backward, but I cannot perceive him. On the left hand, where he doth work, but I cannot behold him; he hideth himself on his right hand, that I cannot see him. But he knoweth the way that I take; when he hath tried me, I shall come forth as gold." Job was a traveler lost in the darkness; a frustrated man, apparently mystified and despondent. It mattered not what he did, or where he went, he encountered increasing problems. When he looked in all directions, poor Job saw everything was bad. Yet, when he looked *up*, his view was clear. He knew that when his ordeal ended, he would be wonderfully compensated. He said: "I shall come forth as gold." "And the LORD turned the captivity of Job, when he prayed for his friends: also the LORD gave Job twice as much as he had before" (Job 42:10).

Even in his darkest moments Job saw a beckoning light at the end of his tunnel. Probably, his terrible sufferings exceeded anything known among men. His friends misunderstood the reasons for his plight; his wife urged him to commit suicide, and for a long time, even God appeared to be indifferent. Yet, Job's faith never wavered. When he emerged triumphantly from his ordeal, he would have agreed with Paul's statement that even unpleasant things could be the messengers of God's infinite care.

Jonah . . . *From Pouting to Preaching* (Jonah 2:7-9)

Jonah was probably the only evangelist who did not desire converts! The prospect of leading a city to repentance was unattractive, for he feared future repercussions would devastate Israel. When, in spite of everything, the people of Nineveh were forgiven, the prophet complained and said: ". . . O LORD , was not this my saying, when I was yet in my country. Therefore I fled before unto Tarshish: for I knew that thou art a gracious God, and merciful, slow to anger, and of great kindness, and repentest thee of the evil. Therefore now, O LORD, take, I beseech thee, my life from me; for it is better for me to die than to live" (see Jonah 4:2). Jonah's flight could have been disastrous for according to the laws of God, a watchman who refused to warn a city of impending danger would be held accountable for the death of the citizens (Ezek. 33:6).

The prophet's disobedience and subsequent flight to Tarshish were overruled to supply additional evidence that the Lord could make all things work together for good to God's children. When Jonah eventually went to Nineveh he said: "Yet forty days, and Nineveh shall be overthrown." He never preached a sermon; he held no organized evangelistic meetings, but the people of "an exceeding great city proclaimed a fast, and put on sackcloth from the greatest of them even to the least of them" (Jonah 3:4-5). Actually this was a more astounding miracle than was seen on the day of Pentecost. The Ninevites worshiped the fish-god, and Jonah's body provided evidence of his strange incarceration. The people believed he had come back from the dead, and his physical appearance supported that conclusion. It is extremely doubtful if the prophet's limited ministry would have been successful had he not carried upon his person the evidence of his being swallowed by the great fish. (See the author's book *Bible Gems*, pages 75-76, published by Kregel Publications, Grand Rapids, Michigan.) It is wonderful to know that even when our stupidity gets us into trouble, the Lord is still able to make those misfortunes work together for our good.

John . . . *From Prison to Praise* (Revelation 1:9)

"I John, who also am your brother, and companion in tribulation, and in the kingdom and patience of Jesus Christ, was in the isle that is called Patmos, for the word of God, and for the testimony of Jesus Christ." When the apostle was banished to the island, many of his friends concluded his ministry had terminated; he would never be seen again. They could not have known that God was opening a door to wider areas of service. Paul, the evangelist, traveled thousands of miles, but the book John was commissioned to write was destined to go around the world.

I have been inside the small cave in which, so it is claimed, John wrote his famous book, but it seemed impossible that from so secluded a pulpit, his message could be heard by all nations. Confined within his prison, the apostle looked into the heavens and saw the four and twenty elders seated around the throne, and the glorious day when the Savior would re-enter the world to be acclaimed King of Kings and Lord of Lords. Had John been permitted to continue his ministry among the churches, he may never have found time to write anything! It was obvious that God never closed one door without opening another. Every cloud has a silver lining, and out of the darkest one comes the greatest shower of blessing.

> Enough, this covers all my wants;
> And so I rest;
> For what I cannot, He can see,
> And in His care I safe shall be
> For ever blest!

THE GREATEST PURCHASE
EVER MADE! (1 CORINTHIANS 6:20; 7:23)

After all conquests made by the armies of Caesar, long lines of chained captives were taken to Rome either to become slaves or to be executed. Notorious enemies were put to death, but others were sold at auctions. During the early history of the Jewish people, there was a law which enabled a blood relation to redeem, rescue or deliver any kinsman who had become a slave. The slave-market was an establishment recognized throughout the ancient world. The citizens of Corinth were aware of this fact, for Roman warships were often seen in which prisoners worked in the galleys. Captives were sometimes seen marching to the ships which took them to perpetual bondage. Slavery has been abolished, but it is difficult to forget the ruthless traders who terrorized the tribes in Africa. The conscience of the world was aroused by the helpless people who were compelled to leave their homeland to become the slaves of strangers. This practice was known to the Corinthian people; they understood clearly what was meant when Paul said: "For ye are bought with a price."

A Terrible Predicament . . . *". . . sold under sin"*
   (Rom. 7:14)

The expression "Ye were bought" suggested a slave market where unfortunate captives sat dejectedly. Corinth was an infamous city in which corruption was predominant. Prior to the arrival of Paul, people did whatever they desired, and repentance was unknown. The missionary constantly reminded his readers that Christianity provided a salvation which was unobtainable apart from Jesus of Nazareth. Condemned by law, and helpless to resist, they were facing a future without hope. Chains reminded them of their bondage, and fear of the future revealed the uncertainty of their souls. They had been ". . . without Christ . . . having no hope, and without God in the world" (Eph. 2:12). The plight of a slave might be summarized under three headings. *Without help; without hope; without happiness.*

   (1) *Without help.* Slaves had no friends; they were strangers

far from home. Some had been warriors, but their resentment continued as they awaited their fate. Young women faced an ignominious future. Rich and lustful men stared at the maidens, and it was easy to understand their thoughts. The captives were helpless as corks tossed on an ocean. They had become victims of circumstances beyond their control. Prior to the auction, prospective buyers examined the slaves who had lost interest in living. It was not important to whom they would be sold; the future could only be a nightmare of horrors. Men would feel the lash of whips, and the women would suffer indignities worse than death.

(2) *Without hope.* It was inconceivable that their night of despair could be followed by a radiant dawn. They were outcasts who resembled lepers banished from society; they had no choice in deciding their future. When slaves considered these things, their outlook remained bleak. The possibility that a kindly benefactor might purchase them was beyond comprehension. They believed they were destined to remain in bondage until they died and were forgotten by everybody.

Paul was a great preacher; he knew how to apply these details to the Christians in Corinth. They had lived sinful lives, ignoring the consequences. Evil passions subjugated their souls; they were addicted to evil, and had no deliverer. Constantly, they yielded to the cravings of sin, and everything indicated this would continue until death. Beyond that event, the Corinthians were unable to see. They would die and be buried, and enter eternity unprepared for what might be there. If the slaves had been wealthy, they might have purchased their freedom — but they were penniless. Had they been exceedingly strong, they might have snapped their chains — but they were weak. If they had influential friends in Caesar's palace, they might have been assisted in their quest for liberty, but they were strangers in a strange land; they were alone and helpless.

(3) *Without happiness.* The ancient Hebrews would have appreciated the predicament of people to be sold. Some Jews had been captives in Babylon where they were requested to sing some of the songs of their homeland. The psalmist wrote: "By the rivers of Babylon, there we sat down, yea, we wept,

when we remembered Zion. We hanged our harps upon the willows in the midst thereof. For there they that carried us away captive required of us a song; and they that wasted us required of us mirth, saying, Sing us one of the songs of Zion. How shall we sing the LORD's song in a strange land?" (Ps. 137:1-4). Esau was unable to sing after he had exchanged his birthright for a bowl of lentil soup. He became a slave to his appetite (Gen. 25:33-34 and Heb. 12:16-17). Simon Peter could not sing after he had denied his Lord. He was a slave of his fear, and went out into the night to weep bitterly (Luke 22:62). Judas would have been completely out-of-tune had he tried to sing after betraying the Lord; he forged the chains which bound him eternally (Matt. 27:3-5). A slave market was a night without stars!

A Tremendous Price . . . *"Christ . . . gave himself a ransom for all"* (1 Tim. 2:6)

The market place of the world was filled with excitement; even the prisoners wondered what was happening. The prospective buyers were in their places; the auctioneer was waiting to begin the sale; the fate of the captives was about to be decided. Then, suddenly, a Stranger entered the auction room. He was different from all others; He was calm; His appearance was dignified, and His face displayed eagerness to participate in the bidding. If imagination may be permitted to describe the scene, then if one asked: "Sir, do you wish to purchase a slave?", the Stranger calmly repied: "No, I have no desire to buy a slave. I wish to purchase all of them." Then someone said: "Sir, all the money in the world could not make such a purchase." "That is correct, but I possess everything. Nevertheless, I have no desire to continue their slavery; I wish to set them free." If Paul ever described that fascinating scene, he finished with the announcement: "And the Stranger's name was Jesus, and 'If the Son therefore shall make you free, ye shall be free indeed'" (John 8:36).

Four of the happiest years of my life were spent in South Africa where I was the national evangelist of the Baptist Churches. I preached to white people, Indians, Africans and the wonderful colored people of Cape Province. As I mingled with these people I was taught many things. I was intrigued by the native custom of buying wives. Within the African culture, a man is required to purchase his wives, and the price for each one is ten cows, plus one fat cow—as a bonus gift for the mother-in-law. One day I talked with the native servant of a Baptist minister in Natal. I said: "Sam, do you plan to be married some day?" He replied, "Yes, Baas, I sure do." "How much will you pay for your wife?" "Ten cows, Master—plus one extra for her mother." "Sam," I continued, "What if you married the daughter of a minister. How much would that cost?" "Twelve cows—plus one." Then I asked: "What if you wanted to marry the daughter of a chief? How much would you have to pay then?" Suddenly, the fellow's eyes rolled upward as he answered: "Oh, Baas, fifty cows—plus one." That delightful African laughed when I said: "Sam, you pay for your wife before you get her." "That is so, Master." "We white people are different. We get our wives for nothing, but we pay for the rest of our lives!" His eyes shone when he said: "Yes, Baas; yes, Baas, yes, Baas."

Afterward I said: "Sam, I know somebody else Who had to buy his bride, but He gave much more than ten, twelve, or even fifty cows. Do you know His name?" Samuel's eyes became pools of delight when he replied: "Yes, I know His name. Jesus gave all that He had — even His precious blood." I knew then that Samuel was another who had been "bought with a price!" The biblical doctrines of redemption are so challenging, that even the greatest thinkers have been unable to exhaust their meanings, but three simple headings might explain some of their mysteries.

(1) *The Compelling Task.* The redemption of kinsmen was one of the best known Jewish laws. It was restricted to members of a family. No person could demand the release of a slave unless he were a member of the slave's family (see Leviticus 25:47-49). That law presented problems when God desired to redeem sinners. The Almighty did not belong to the human race; He was Divine; people were human. Therefore, it was considered necessary that Jehovah, in some strange way, would become "bone of our bone, and flesh of our flesh." This was

accomplished when through the Incarnation the Son of God was made in the likeness of men. Only then did He become eligible to participate in the redemption of sinful people. His action speaks eloquently of the motivating reasons behind the decision to attempt what He did. The laying aside of His glory; the descent to earth, the ensuing temptations and suffering were overcome by the greatness of His resolve to complete what He commenced. After considering all these facts, the poet wrote: "How greatly Jesus must have loved us." The apostle John wrote: "For God *so* loved the world . . ." (John 3:16). Divine love is immeasurable. The love of Christ overcame every challenge made against it.

(2) *The Completed Transaction.* Within an eastern slave-market the liberation of a slave was visible for all to witness. When the worth of the human produce was established, the redeemer or purchaser paid whatever was required, and from that moment ownership was transferred from the seller to the buyer. It is difficult to interpret these facts. For example, the question might be asked: "To whom did Christ pay the redemption requirements?" When writing to Timothy, Paul said: "Who (Christ) gave himself a ransom for all . . ." (1 Tim. 2:6). The New Testament teaches that the Lord redeemed us with His blood—but to whom was the debt paid? Many affirm that since sinners had broken the laws of God, the debt was dischargeable to the Almighty; that appeasement was made whereby sinful man could be exonerated and pardoned. Others believe that since men had become the slaves of Satan, the purchase price was the legal way by which even the prince of evil had to acknowledge God was justified in demanding the release of captives. Theological arguments could continue indefinitely, but the fact remained that what Christ accomplished through His death was the guarantee that all who know the power of His redeeming love will never again become slaves.

At the end of the Battle of Britain during World War II, Winston Churchill declared: "Never have so many owed so much to so few." His statement could be paraphrased to read: "Never have so many owed so much to one Man—Who died to bring us to God." Christ gave all that He possessed to set us

176

free. This truth was expressed through His parables. He said: "And again the kingdom of heaven is like unto treasure hid in a field; the which when a man hath found, he hideth, and for joy thereof goeth and selleth all that he hath, and buyeth that field. Again the kingdom of heaven is like unto a merchant man, seeking goodly pearls: Who, when he had found one pearl of great price, went and sold all that he had, and bought it" (Matt. 13:44-46).

(3) *The Commanding Triumph.* The writer to the Hebrews wrote: ". . . Jesus the author and finisher of our faith, who for the joy that was set before him, endured the cross, despising the shame, and is set down at the right hand of the throne of God" (Heb. 12:2). Perhaps even slaves found it difficult to comprehend the importance of the transaction completed before them. The transfer of ownership could mean going out of the frying pan into the fire! The second master might be worse than the first. Yet, if and when the new owner offered unlimited freedom and sufficient help to assist the liberated slave in his new experience, the redemption suggested became unbelievable. How could any man clad in fine garments be considerate to a slave dressed in rags? Why should a rich man desire to provide sustenance for a beggar? Jesus said: "I am the bread of life: he that cometh to me shall never hunger, and he that believeth on me shall never thirst" (John 6:35). The greatest evidence for Christ and His message is the power that transforms slaves into princes and princesses. Hannah, the mother of Samuel, expressed this wonderful fact when she said: "He raiseth up the poor out of the dust, and lifteth up the beggar from the dunghill, to set them among princes, and to make them inherit the throne of glory" (1 Sam.1 2:8).

A Thrilling Privilege . . . *"glorify God in your body"* (1 Cor. 6:20)

The Christians in Rome understood what Paul meant when he wrote: "I beseech you therefore, by the mercies of God, that ye present your bodies a living sacrifice, holy, acceptable unto God, which is your reasonable service" (Rom. 12:1). The novelist Lewis Wallace (1827-1905) wrote the very popular book

Ben Hur, in which he described the life of Judah Ben-Hur. Sentenced to work in the galley of a Roman warship, Judah eventually saved the life of the officer in charge of the sinking vessel and was rewarded by adoption into one of the most famous families in Rome. Wallace described the faithful allegiance of the one-time slave to his illustrious foster-father. It might be interesting to know if that author ever found inspiration in the New Testament.

Paul described the plight of the slaves, and appealed for sincere service to be rendered to their Heavenly Benefactor. Since the Son of God did so much for man, it was to be expected that all redeemed slaves render grateful allegiance to the new Master. The apostle emphasized that this was reasonable service. That is, it was a way to liquidate some of the debt owned to Christ. He gave His all for us; we are expected to give our best to Him. The reason for our desire to serve the Lord may be explained under three headings.

(1) *We serve Him to Express Gratitude.* Without the redemptive power of the love of Christ, everybody would still be in chains! "For when we were yet without strength, in due time Christ died for the ungodly" (Rom. 5:6). Without strength meant incapability to gain our freedom. Another had to work on our behalf. As a seriously ill person, restored by the skill of a devoted doctor remains grateful to his physician, so Christians raised to newness of life should never forget the Great Physician.

(2) *We serve Him to Experience Grace . . . sufficient for every need.* The world into which a liberated slave entered was not always an easy place in which to live. Temptations abounded, and other traders might try to take them back into bondage. The secret of successful living was found in proximity to the Redeemer. He Who liberated us in the first place, made it possible for people to stay close to Him; to live in His presence; to feed at His table, and draw upon His resources. Writing to the Corinthians, Paul said: "There hath no temptation taken you but such as is common to man: but God is faithful, who will not suffer you to be tempted above that ye are able; but will with the temptation, also make a way to escape, that ye may be able

to bear it" (1 Cor. 10:13). The struggles of a baby bird to emerge from an egg strengthens it for future requirements. Likewise, the problems of life sometimes are channels of blessing by which we are enabled to overcome the difficulties of tomorrow.

(3) *We serve Him to Enjoy Gladness.* As it becomes impossible to forget the past, so it is increasingly difficult to ignore the future. To help the Redeemer emancipate others in bondage to drugs, alcohol and other evils, is among the greatest privileges of life. To see appreciation in the eyes of the afflicted, and recognize our Lord's approval, provides a gladness for which there is no substitute. Paul said: "For we are laborers together with God . . ." (1 Cor. 3:9). He is never far away.

Frederick Barton, in his entrancing book, *One Hundred Great Texts and Their Treatment,* tells the story of an elderly colored Christian who attended a despondent master. She asked: "Massa, does yo see de bright side dis morning?" "No, Nanny, it is not as bright as I wish it." She replied: "Well, Massa, I allus see de bright side." He replied: "You do! maybe, you haven't had much trouble." "Maybe not," she answered, and then she went on to describe what had taken place when she lived in Virginia. Her children had been auctioned one by one, her husband had been sold, and finally she herself had become a slave. She had never heard from any one of her family. She concluded by saying, "Maybe I ain't seen no trouble." The man replied: "But, Nanny, have you seen the bright side all the time?" "Allus, massa, allus." "Then how did you do it?" Her reply was eloquent. "Dis is the way, Massa. When I see de black cloud coming over," and she waved her dark hand inside the tent, as though one might be settling down there, "and it 'pears like its crushin' down on me, den, I just whips aroun' on de oder side, an I find de Lord Jesus dar, and den it's all bright and cl'ar. Da bright side's allus where Jesus is."

All religions, when contrasted with Christianity, leave much to be desired. Their teachings cannot be compared with the doctrines of Christ, and are unable to satisfy the need of a human heart. That might have been one of the reasons why the writer to the Hebrews repeatedly used the word "better." During the first century the Jews were overwhelmed; their temple destroyed, and their hope shattered. Many young Christians were in danger of losing their faith, and to encourage and console such people, the letter to the Hebrews was written. It explains that Christ excelled anything which had been lost. The word "better" was used thirteen times for the epistle mentioned a better hope; testament; covenant; promises, sacrifice; country and finally, a better resurrection. The writer emphasized that although many things had apparently been lost, Christ remained and surpassed anything they had known. Nevertheless, the truths taught in the epistle can be seen more clearly in the daily life of the Savior.

An Increasing Pleasure . . . His Wine Was Better
   (John 2:9-10)

". . . the governor of the feast called the bridegroom, And saith unto him: Every man at the beginning doth set forth good wine; and when men have well drunk, then that which is worse: BUT THOU HAST KEPT THE GOOD WINE UNTIL NOW."

Eastern weddings were prolonged times of rejoicing; the festivities continued for several days. It would appear from the text that Mary was a friend of the happy couple, and was invited with Jesus and His followers to celebrate the happy event. It has been suggested that the presence of the disciples imposed a strain on the supplies of wine, and Mary assumed the responsibility for the shortage. To prevent embarrassment for her friends, she confided in Jesus and the problem was quickly solved. It was significant that the governor of the feast expressed amazement at the quality of the new wine. It is difficult to decide whether this practice hid the stinginess of the host, or the incapability of drunkards to recognize cheap refreshments. Much has been written about the wedding at Cana, but for the purpose of this study, it is sufficient to emphasize that anything produced by the Savior was better than the world could offer.

During World War II a thousand marines sat on a South Pacific Island listening to a gospel message which was accompanied by the sound of gun-fire in the distance. When the Chaplain concluded his sermon, one of the marines sang the closing hymn. As the shell scarred palms swayed nearby, more than half of the company came forward to profess their faith in Christ. The marine soloist, a former opera singer, sang:

> I'd rather have Jesus than silver or gold:
> I'd rather be His than have riches untold
> I'd rather have Jesus than houses or land,
> I'd rather be led by His nail-pierced hand.
>
> Than to be the king of a vast domain
> Or be held in sin's dread sway:
> I'd rather have Jesus than anything
> This world affords today.
>
> George Beverly Shea
>
> (Quoted from *101 More Hymn Stories*, Kenneth W. Osbeck, Kregel Publications, Grand Rapids, MI)

An Inspired Presentation . . . *His Teaching Was Better* (John 14:8-9)

"Philip saith unto him, Lord, shew us the Father, and it sufficeth us. Jesus saith unto him, Have I been so long time with you, and yet hast thou not known me, Philip? he that hath seen me hath seen the Father; and how sayest thou then, Shew us the Father?"

One of the most appealing stories ever told from a pulpit concerns the little boy who was afraid of the dark. When his mother reminded her child that God was with him, the lad replied, "I know God is with me, but I like somebody with skin on!" Long ago, Philip was apprehensive. He had heard his Master speaking about the Father, but everything appeared to be vague. He had heard about God and knew the scriptures referred to Jehovah. Yet, Jesus appeared to possess intimate knowledge of the Almighty and the disciple desired that things be explained more clearly. When Jesus assured Philip that he had already seen the Father, things became more confusing than ever. The disciple had yet to learn that Jesus was God—with skin on! The Almighty had come to earth and had walked among men. People who listened to Jesus heard the voice of God; those who looked at the Savior saw the face of Jehovah. Philip could not comprehend the lesson being taught; like us—he was an immature student!

The New Testament supplies many examples of the excellence of Christ's teaching, but probably His references to sparrows are among the most inspiring. The Lord said: "Are not two sparrows sold for a farthing? and one of them shall not fall on the ground without your Father (seeing it)" (Matt. 10:29). He also said: "Are not five sparrows sold for two farthings, and not one of them is forgotten before God?" (Luke 12:6). A sparrow was an insignificant bird, unworthy of being used in the temple sacrifices. It was considered to be almost worthless and was sold two for a farthing—one of the smallest coins in Palestine. When a customer bought four birds, one extra was given without additional payment. That little bird was so valued by the Almighty, that one of its kind could not fall to the ground in India, China, Africa, or any other part of the world without the fact being known to the Lord. Such a revelation of divine kindness had never before been given. Jehovah had been an almost mystical Deity, and the idea that He was a Father to be loved and trusted was a truth men failed to grasp. God saw greatness in simple things. Jesus said: ". . . Consider the lilies of the field, how they grow; they toil not, neither do they spin: And yet I say unto you, That even Solomon in all his glory was not arrayed like one of these" (Matt. 6:28-29). Jesus revealed that God so loved—that He could hold children in His arms. The teaching of Jesus surpassed anything ever heard.

An Infinite Patience . . . *His Attitude Was Better*
  (John 8:11)
  Jesus practiced what He preached, and this was never more

182

apparent than when a sinful woman was pushed into His presence. Her accusers said: "Master this woman was taken in adultery, in the very act. Now Moses in the law commanded us, that such should be stoned: but what sayest thou?" (John 8:4-5). They were not concerned about the woman's immorality. They were schemers who planned to arrest the Savior, and if the woman's execution could enhance their chances of success, they would have stoned her immediately. The scribes and Pharisees were cynical, merciless and vicious. The Lord was more gracious for when He was left alone with the adulteress, He said: ". . . where are those thine accusers? hath no man condemned thee? She said: No man, Lord. And Jesus said unto her, Neither do I condemn thee: go and sin no more." The Savior was exceedingly gentle. His attitude resembled refreshing rain after a drought; sunshine after an ice storm; kindness after criticism.

The early church fathers refused to include this story in their sacred writings for they feared it would encourage immorality. They failed to understand that when the woman said "Lord" she did so by the enabling power of the Holy Spirit; her faith had brought pardon. Jesus had already forgotten her past, forgiven her sin, and was offering advice concerning her future (1 Cor. 12:3). The Savior was different from all other teachers. Those who looked into His face saw the heart of God.

An Infallible Promise . . . His Gift Was Better (Rom. 6:23)

It is an interesting fact that although the Egyptian magicians emulated the example of Moses (Exod. 7:11-12), no person ever accomplished what Christ did. The Savior honored all His commitments. He fed thousands of hungry people, healed all kinds of diseases, but His greatest promise concerned the possession of eternal life. Jesus said to Martha of Bethany: "I am the resurrection and the life; he that believeth in me, though he were dead, yet shall he live; and whosoever liveth and believeth in me shall never die . . ." (John 11:25-26). Death is the greatest enemy of mankind, and even the best of human efforts are destined to end in a grave. Science may delay the inevitable, but even the most illustrious benefactors of mankind die. They bequeath their works to posterity, but their sojourn on earth is limited. Millions of dollars are being spent in the hope of increasing longevity, but unfortunately mortality terminates in death. It was amazing that Jesus gave everlasting life to all who sought it. It should be remembered that He spoke of *eternal* life. Doctors may relieve pain, and under certain circumstances, restart the beating of a heart, but even the most renowned surgeon cannot give eternal life.

An Incomparable Presence . . . *His Company Was Better* (Luke 24:30-32)

The journey had ended, but the two travelers were uneasy. Their Companion had said "Goodbye" and was leaving. "But they constrained him, saying, Abide with us, for it is toward evening, and the day is far spent. And he went in to tarry with them" (Luke 24:29). Those people had been away from home for at least a week, and, possibly were unprepared for an overnight guest. At that time of the evening it would have been difficult to obtain provisions. They could have managed with a snack, but something more substantial would have been needed for the Stranger.

Nothing is known of the house into which Jesus was invited. It might have been spacious or small, but although it might have seemed unwise to extend an invitation to their fellow-traveler, *they constrained Him* to enter their home. The Lord probably said he had no desire to impose upon their generosity, but they had been captivated by His conversation, and thrilled with His company. They had walked the road to and from Jerusalem many times, but had never known such fellowship. Their Companion was well-informed, courteous and charming. He knew the scriptures, and what He said made sense! They desired to know more, and any inconvenience would be worthwhile, if they could prolong the fellowship known on the highway. After leaving their pessimistic colleagues, it had been delightful to listen to the Stranger's exposition of the sacred writings.

Hastily the meal was prepared, and then "He took bread, and

184

blessed it, and break it, and gave to them" (verse 30). They stared at their Guest and remembered other hands had done a similar thing. When the nail prints became visible, ". . . he was known of them in breaking of bread" (Luke 24:35). Suddenly they were looking at an empty chair, for He had "vanished out of their sight. And they said one to another, Did not our heart burn within us, while he talked with us by the way, and while he opened to us the scriptures?" (Luke 24:32). The disciples never forgot that wonderful experience; they had walked and talked with the risen Son of God. Many others have proved that fellowship with Christ is better than anything else on earth. It is refreshing to remember that Jesus said: "Go ye therefore and teach all nations . . . and lo, *I am with you alway even unto the end of the world*" (Matt. 28:19-20). It is wonderful to believe on Him; better to walk with Him, but best of all to see Him face to face at the end of our pilgrimage. "And they shall see his face" (Rev. 22:4).

> He speaks, and the sound of His voice,
> Is so sweet, the birds hush their singing.
> And the melody, that He gives to me,
> Within my heart is ringing.

> And He walks with me, and He talks with me,
> And He tells me I am His own:
> And the joy we share as we tarry there,
> None other has ever known.

Scripture Text Index

GENESIS
3 5
11:1-4 10
25:33-34 174
28:12-13 9
28:16-21 . .167, 168
35:22 14
37:26-27 15
45:5-8 168
49:1, 2 14
49:3-4 14
49:8-10 15
49:13-17 17
49:20 18
49:22-24 21
49:22-26 19
49:24 24
49:25 20

EXODUS
14:26-27 35
21:21-32 134
31:10 85
32:19-32 . . . .66, 67

LEVITICUS
25:47-49 175

NUMBERS
14:6-9 32
15:1-10 165

JUDGES
16:16-17 67
18:27-31 18

1 SAMUEL
2:17 125
7:10 35
12:8 177
16:7 109

17:45-46 32
25:37 36

2 SAMUEL
19:34-37 . . . .41, 42

1 KINGS
11:28 31
18:45 38
19:19 26
19:21 27

2 KINGS
2:9 . . . . .27, 28
2:11 12
4:19-36 29
4:42-44 29
5:10-14 29
6:20 29
7:6-7 35
13:3 31
13:20-21 29

2 CHRONICLES
13:13-15 32
13:15-17 33
13:18 30

JOB
1:8 43
3:11-17 43
14:14 43
19:26-27 44
23:8-10 169
42:10 169

PSALMS
1:1-3 36
17:15 41
42:1 56
46:4 39
84:11 40

104:16-17 36
105:17-22 168
115:12 93
115—118 92
116:12, 17 93
119:105 54
121:1-2 38
133:1-3 103
136:23-25 92, 94, 95
137:1-4 174
139:7-10 25
144:15 34
145:3 47
146:5-7 56

ECCLESIASTES
3:7 . . . . . . .60, 101
11:3 37

ISAIAH
6:8 69
9:6-7 82
12:2-3 40
61:3 85

JEREMIAH
2:13 84

EZEKIEL
22:30 66
33:6 170
47:7-9 38

DANIEL
9:25-26 140

JOEL
2:23-27 . . . . .39, 40

JONAH
2:7-9 169
3:4-5 170

4:2 170

MICAH
3:8 39

ZECHARIAH
4:6 29
9:9 106

MALACHI
4:2 44

MATTHEW
5:6 56
5:44 16
6:21 83
6:28-29 182
8:2-3 22
9:28 70
10:1 133
10:29 182
11:21 102
11:28 ..53, 57, 142
12:43-45 70
13:44-46 177
14:1-2 132
14:29-30 136
14:30-31 21
15:26 84
15:29 109
15:30 75
15:32-39 29
16:9-10 29
16:26 102
17:5 88
17:14-16 78
17:19 27
19:24 75
20:30-34 70
22:3-6 82
22:2, 11-13 81
22:8-10 84
26:14-15 134

26:30 89
27:3-5 ....133, 174
28:20 87
28:19-20 ..105, 185

MARK
5:24 99
5:38-43 98
5:43 98
7:32-37 .98, 99, 101
8:22-25 .....22, 23
8:22-26 ...98, 101
9:9 102
10:16 25
10:17-23 113
11:7 106
11:24 35
12:28-34 112
12:41-44 ..108, 109
14:50 49
14:67-68 131
16:15 .....68, 143

LUKE
1:15 127
1:31 118
5:5-8 ....75, 76
5:19 77
7:15 29
7:22-23 ...128, 138
7:24, 28 128
8:30 73
8:37-39 104
9:10-17 102
9:30-31 ...103, 104
9:57-62 ...160, 161
10:17-24 145
10:38-42 79
12:6 182
12:18-20 149
13:11-13 23
16:19-31 134

16:22-23 12
17:12-18 70
17:21 112
18:35-43 29
19:3 138
19:6 76
19:8 139
19:35-41 106
19:37-40 148
19:42-44 106
22:62 174
23:32 115
23:42-43 12
23:46 91
24:29-35 ..184, 185

JOHN
1:11 55
1:29 127
1:50-51 11
2:9-10 180
3:2 ......139, 140
3:16 ...29, 94, 176
3:30 127
4:6 107
4:29-30 141
4:40-42 141
6:32-35 57
6:35 177
7:39 26
8:4-11 182-183
8:6-9 130
8:36 174
10:11 52
10:27 52
10:27-29 ...24, 146
11:3 79
11:25-26 183
12:7 80
12:9-11 99
12:20-23 136
12:21 102

188

12:22 137
12:23-24 137
13:30 .....63, 134
14:2 54
14:6 ...11, 87, 141
14:8-9 181
14:13-14 119
14:12, 16 28
15:11 39
16:7 74
20:19-20 ..143, 147

ACTS
1:4-8 28
3:4-8 50
3:4-16 ....120, 121
4:12 ......11, 86
4:33 49
4:32-35 50
5:34-40 ...113, 114
5:38-40 114
7:9-10 149
7:55-56 110
7:58 68
8:1 68
8:5-8 144
8:26-28 144
9:1 68
9:13 68
9:13-17 ...149, 150
11:22-24 146
13:13 ......61, 62
13:28-30 ..149, 151
14 53
15:37-41 51
17:23 137, 150, 154
17:32 155
18:1 156
18:4-8 159
18:14-17 159
19:10 ....151, 152
21:4-13 ...162-164

22:21 68
24:16 135
26:28 116
28:30-31 45

ROMANS
1:15 160
1:16 157
1:30-32 18
3:38-39 24
5:6 178
6:4 91
6:23 183
7:14 172
7:14-15 135
7:18-20 73
8:28 167
8:28-29 84
8:31 31
8:38-39 24
12:1 177

1 CORINTHIANS
1:1 159
1:23 155
2:1, 2 ....154, 158
2:7-12 151
3:9 179
6:20 172
7:23 172
10:13 179
12:3 183
15:6 28
15:31 29

2 CORINTHIANS
2:15-16 115
8:2 147
11:23-27 45
11:23-28 167
12:9 ......21, 74

GALATIANS
1:8 49

2:20 29
6:14 159

EPHESIANS
1:4 84
1:10 ......81, 82
2:2-5 152
2:4 47
2:5 48
2:5-7 48
2:8-9 86
2:12 .....84, 172

PHILIPPIANS
1:23 180
2:5-8 .....69, 95
2:10-11 82
2:24-28 152
4:13 73

COLOSSIANS
1:27 73

1 TIMOTHY
1:16 135
2:6 ......174, 176

2 TIMOTHY
4:6-8 .....69, 110,
           164-165
4:7-8 44
4:8 161
4:10 ......62, 126
4:10-11 63
4:20 153

HEBREWS
1:2-3 52
2:3-4 48
4:14-16 .....51, 52
7:22-24 51
9:12-28 52
9:27 87
10:24-25 147

189

11:10 42
11:30-40 145
12:1 136
12:2 . . . . . . .6, 177
12:10 110
12:16-17 174
13:8 . . . . . . .21, 35
13:20-21 52

JAMES
1:17 95
2:20 35

1 PETER
5:2-4 . . . . . . .52, 53
5:5 85

2 PETER
1:4 53
3:13 . . . . . . .53, 55

1 JOHN
2:12 118

3 JOHN
7 121

REVELATION
1:9 . . . . . .170, 171
7:9-17 58
11:15 55
13:8 82
19:7-8 85
21:10-24 . . . .54, 55
21:12 11
21:25-27 55
22:1-2 . . . . . .38, 39
22:4 . . . . . .55, 185

BIBLIOGRAPHY

Amplified New Testament. Zondervan Publishing House, Grand Rapids, 1958.

Barton, F. M. *One Hundred Great Texts and Their Treatment.* Richard E. Smith, New York, 1930.

Englishman's Greek Testament. Samuel Bagster and Company, London, 1877.

Farrar, F. W. *The Life and Work of St. Paul.* Kregel Publications, Grand Rapids, 1981.

Handfulls on Purpose. Wm. B. Eerdmans Publishing Co., Grand Rapids, 1947.

Josephus, Flavius. *The Complete Works of Flavius Josephus.* Kregel Publications, Grand Rapids, 1960.

Osbeck, Kenneth B. *One Hundred and One More Hymn Stories.* Kregel Publications, Grand Rapids, 1985.

Powell, Ivor. *The Amazing Acts.* Kregel Publications, Grand Rapids, 1987.

Powell, Ivor. *Bible Cameos.* Kregel Publications, Grand Rapids, 1985.

Powell, Ivor. *Bible Gems.* Kregel Publications, Grand Rapids, 1987.

Powell, Ivor. *Bible Windows.* Kregel Publications, Grand Rapids, 1985.

Powell, Ivor. *Bible Treasures.* Kregel Publications, Grand Rapids, 1985.

Powell, Ivor. *What in the World Will Happen Next?* Kregel Publications, Grand Rapids, 1985.

Pulpit Commentary. Wm. B. Eerdmans Publishing Co., Grand Rapids, 1950.

Spurgeon, C. H. *Spurgeon on the Psalms.* Kregel Publications, Grand Rapids, 1976.

Tan, P. L. *Encyclopedia of 7700 Illustrations.* Assurance Publishers, Rockville, Maryland, 1979.